PENGUIN CANADA

THE ULTIMATE TFSA GUIDE

GORDON PAPE is Canada's best known financial author and the publisher of five investment newsletters, including *The Income Investor, Mutual Funds Update, The Canada Report,* and *The Internet Wealth Builder.* He is the author of several national bestsellers, including *Tax-Free Savings Accounts, Sleep-Easy Investing,* and *The Retirement Time Bomb,* and has spoken at hundreds of seminars in Canada and the United States. Pape is frequently quoted in the media, and is a popular guest on radio and television shows. His website is located at www.BuildingWealth.ca.

D0878563

Also by Gordon Pape

INVESTMENT ADVICE

Tax-Free Savings Accounts

Sleep-Easy Investing

The Retirement Time Bomb

Get Control of Your Money

6 Steps to $1 Million

Retiring Wealthy in the 21st Century

The Complete Guide to RRIFs and LIFs (with David Tafler)

Gordon Pape's 2004 Buyer's Guide to Mutual Funds (with Eric Kirzner)

Gordon Pape's 2004 Buyer's Guide to RRSPs

Secrets of Successful Investing (with Eric Kirzner)

Gordon Pape's Investing Strategies 2001 (with Richard Croft and Eric Kirzner)

Making Money in Mutual Funds

The Canadian Mortgage Book (with Bruce McDougall)

The Best of Pape's Notes

Head Start (with Frank Jones)

Retiring Wealthy

Building Wealth in the '90s

Low-Risk Investing in the '90s

Low-Risk Investing

Building Wealth

CONSUMER ADVICE

Gordon Pape's International Shopping Advice (with Deborah Kerbel)

HUMOUR

The $50,000 Stove Handle

CHRISTMAS (with Deborah Kerbel)

Quizmas Carols

Family Quizmas

Quizmas: Christmas Trivia Family Fun
(www.quizmas.net)

FICTION (with Tony Aspler)

Chain Reaction

The Scorpion Sanction

The Music Wars

NON-FICTION

Montreal at the Crossroads (with Donna Gabeline and Dane Lanken)

The Ultimate
TFSA
GUIDE

Strategies for Building a
Tax-Free Fortune

GORDON PAPE

PENGUIN
CANADA

PENGUIN CANADA

Published by the Penguin Group

Penguin Group (Canada), 90 Eglinton Avenue East, Suite 700,
Toronto, Ontario, Canada M4P 2Y3 (a division of Pearson Canada Inc.)

Penguin Group (USA) Inc., 375 Hudson Street, New York, New York 10014, U.S.A.
Penguin Books Ltd, 80 Strand, London WC2R 0RL, England
Penguin Ireland, 25 St Stephen's Green, Dublin 2, Ireland (a division of Penguin Books Ltd)
Penguin Group (Australia), 250 Camberwell Road, Camberwell, Victoria 3124, Australia
(a division of Pearson Australia Group Pty Ltd)
Penguin Books India Pvt Ltd, 11 Community Centre, Panchsheel Park,
New Delhi – 110 017, India
Penguin Group (NZ), 67 Apollo Drive, Rosedale, North Shore 0632, New Zealand
(a division of Pearson New Zealand Ltd)
Penguin Books (South Africa) (Pty) Ltd, 24 Sturdee Avenue, Rosebank,
Johannesburg 2196, South Africa

Penguin Books Ltd, Registered Offices: 80 Strand, London WC2R 0RL, England

First published 2010

1 2 3 4 5 6 7 8 9 10   (WEB)

Copyright © Gordon Pape Enterprises Ltd., 2010

Manufactured in Canada.

LIBRARY AND ARCHIVES CANADA CATALOGUING IN PUBLICATION

Pape, Gordon, 1936-
The ultimate TFSA guide : strategies for building a tax-free fortune / Gordon Pape.

Includes bibliographical references and index.
ISBN 978-0-14-317361-8

1. Tax-Free Savings Accounts (Canada). 2. Finance, Personal--Canada.
3. Saving and investment--Canada. 4. Tax planning--Canada. . I. Title.

HG179.P377 2010   332.024'010971   C2009-906284-4

Visit the Penguin Group (Canada) website at **www.penguin.ca**

Special and corporate bulk purchase rates available; please see
www.penguin.ca/corporatesales or call 1-800-810-3104, ext. 2477 or 2474

To my wife, Shirley,
who fought back against tremendous odds
with courage, determination, and dignity.
May you be rewarded with many years of renewed health.

—With love and admiration, Gordon

Contents

Introduction

When I wrote the original *Tax-Free Savings Accounts* in the fall of 2008, the plans had not yet been officially launched, and most people knew very little about them. Now they have been around for a while, but guess what? Most Canadians still know little about them and how they work.

Conceptually, TFSAs are simple. You deposit money into an account and later withdraw it tax-free to use however you wish. Just like bank savings accounts, some might say.

Except they're not! TFSAs are much more complex than they first appear, as proven by the hundreds of questions I have received since *Tax-Free Savings Accounts* was published in early 2009.

Moreover, some of the key elements of the program have evolved since the plan was originally unveiled by Finance Minister Jim Flaherty in his 2008 budget. The Canada Revenue Agency has interpreted some of the tax rules differently than originally envisaged by the Department of Finance. Issues relating to the cross-border treatment of the plans have emerged. Succession rules have been put into place by the provinces. Financial institutions have launched a wide range of plans, in some cases leaving people confused about what they can and can't invest in.

This book addresses all these topics and provides up-to-date answers. My staff and I have also gathered as much information as we could about the many different plans available, which you will find summarized in Chapter 14.

In Chapter 15, I have included a wide range of TFSA questions from readers with my answers. If after digesting all this information you are still uncertain about something, send your own question to me at Gordon.Pape@BuildingWealth.ca and type "TFSA book question" in the subject line. I can't provide personal answers, but replies to selected questions will be posted on www.BuildingWealth.ca and www.TFSAbook.com.

Tax-Free Savings Accounts are a great new way to build personal wealth but they need to be used properly. I hope this book will help you to achieve that.

1

The Beginning: Budget 2008

No one expected much when Finance Minister Jim Flaherty stood up to give his Budget Speech in the House of Commons at 4 P.M. on February 26, 2008.

The cupboard was pretty much bare. The Conservative government, anticipating an early election, had dipped deeply into the nation's dwindling surplus the previous October, when Flaherty had delivered an Economic Statement that was actually a mini-budget in very thin disguise.

At that time, the finance minister had announced a second cut in the Goods and Services Tax (GST), reducing it to 5 percent, as the Tories had promised during their election campaign. He had announced a reduction of half a percentage point in the lowest-tier income tax rate. He had increased personal tax exemptions across the board for all Canadians. He had cut the rates on Employment Insurance. He had announced deep cuts to the federal corporate tax rate, slashing it from 22.1 percent to 15 percent by 2012.

The total cost of all those tax goodies was estimated at a whopping $188.1 billion over the next six fiscal years. Of that,

$72.7 billion was eaten up by the GST cut, $64.9 billion went to income tax savings, and $50.5 billion to the corporate tax cuts.

But after handing out all those goodies, the Conservatives discovered the opposition parties were in no mood to force an election. Instead, they went along with every measure presented to them by the government, thwarting Stephen Harper's plans for an early election.

That left the government with no choice but to bring in a new budget. No one expected much. In the days leading up to the speech, the media talked about green initiatives, municipal infrastructure, more aid to students, and minor tinkering with the GST. Yawners all!

So, when Flaherty rose to speak, expectations were low and the public was largely uninterested. He attempted to change that right off the top.

"Mr. Speaker," he intoned in the usual formality of the House of Commons, "the budget is balanced. Taxes have been cut. And Canadians will now have a powerful new incentive to save money, tax-free: the Tax-Free Savings Account that we are announcing today."[1]

Tax-Free Savings Accounts (TFSAs), which no one had previously thought much about, were suddenly centre stage in the most important parliamentary event of the year.

From there, the minister droned on about the strength of the Canadian economy and all the great things the Conservatives had done for taxpayers since taking office in February 2006. He was about one-third of the way through the Budget Speech when he returned to the only major new initiative he had to offer.

"If we are to help families prepare for the long term, we must ensure Canadians have the right incentives to save for the future," he said. "Saving isn't always easy. But it's important. Unfortunately, for too long, government punished people who did the right thing.

"As one of my constituents recently said to me: 'I go to work. I collect my pay. I pay my taxes. And after I pay my expenses each month, I try to put some money away. I don't have a lot. But I am reaching my goal.

"'Yet, the federal government taxes me on what I earn on my savings and my investments. Savings and investments I socked away with after-tax income. Why am I being punished for doing the right thing?'

"Mr. Speaker, he's right. And we're going to change that.

"The Government will unveil the single most important personal savings vehicle since the introduction of the RRSP: the Tax-Free Savings Account. This flexible, registered, general-purpose account will allow Canadians to watch their savings grow, tax-free.

"It's the first account of its kind in Canadian history."

Flaherty offered a few examples of how the new program would benefit ordinary Canadians. It will, he suggested, help young people save for their first car or their first home. It will help seniors "stretch their retirement savings further."

In fact, TFSAs will allow "every Canadian to set aside a bit of cash each month for a special project, to help their kids, or to simply treat themselves."[2]

Best of all, the program will not cost much, at least initially. In the accompanying Budget Papers, the Department of Finance estimated that TFSAs will cost Ottawa only $5 million in lost revenue in the 2008–2009 fiscal year—a mere pittance.

The program will gradually become more expensive over time: $50 million in forgone revenue in 2009–2010, rising to $385 million by 2012–2013. But that is still just a drop in the bucket for a government that collects more than $240 billion in annual revenue.

Eventually, some 20 years down the road, TFSAs will cost Ottawa an estimated $3 billion annually. But that will be a problem for some future finance minister to deal with.

First reactions to the new savings plan were tepid for the most part. Media reports tended to focus on the economic aspects of the budget and on the comment by then Liberal leader Stéphane Dion that his party might vote against it and bring down the government. (He quickly backed off that position.)

The *National Post* was one of the few newspapers to highlight the TFSA program, calling it "the major budget surprise." However, the *Post* commented that it was "only one of a grab bag of relatively inexpensive goodies."

Jeff Rubin, who at the time was chief economist of CIBC World Markets, said that making TFSAs the star attraction of the budget was "bizarre." He told the *Post*, "It was really trivial. They are forecasting a $50-million tax expenditure next year for three-and-a-half million taxpayers. It works out to $14 per person … [that] doesn't seem to me to be what the centre piece of a budget should be. You have to have something sexy in there."[3]

(Seven months later, CIBC published a report that predicted TFSAs would generate $20 billion worth of business for Bay Street in 2009 and $115 billion in five years.[4])

Over at *The Globe and Mail*, writer Steven Chase suggested that Tax-Free Savings Accounts were "the Tories' attempt to make up for the fact they have not delivered on a poorly drafted 2006 election promise for a tax break on capital gains that would have immediately cost Ottawa billions of dollars annually."[5]

Rob Carrick, personal finance columnist for *The Globe and Mail*, was more enthusiastic, writing, "If the government gets this budget passed, TFSAs will become ubiquitous in a few years. Even though the tax savings aren't dramatic, most households will have at least a few of these plans. The TFSA is the sort of measure you rarely see introduced."[6]

Of course, the budget did pass through Parliament, the regulations were put into place, and now TFSAs are part of our investment options. Most Canadians completely forgot about them in the 10 months between announcement and implementation on January 1, 2009. But now they're here and if you haven't already opened a plan, it's time to start reaping the benefits of this unique program.

2

Some History

The idea of the Tax-Free Savings Account did not spring fully formed from the mind of Finance Minister Jim Flaherty. In fact, his predecessors, Liberal Finance Ministers John Manley and Ralph Goodale, had raised the issue in the 2003 and 2004 budgets with a promise that it would be studied.

In the 2003 budget, the government said it would "examine and consult" on whether what were at the time called Tax-Prepaid Savings Plans (TPSPs) might be "a useful and appropriate additional savings vehicle for Canadians."

In Annex 9 of the 2004 Budget Plan, the government gave the impression that the idea was moving up on the priority list. The document stated,

> Finance officials consulted with interested groups, experts and academics on the tax treatment of savings and TPSPs. The discussions were helpful in gathering views on how the tax treatment of savings could be improved and on TPSPs in particular. The Department is reviewing the views brought forward and is continuing to examine and assess TPSPs and other approaches to improve the tax treatment of savings. In

the consultation, the question of whether a new type of savings plan such as a TPSP could be appropriate for Canada raised a number of important issues which require further consideration.[1]

But there was no reference to the plan in Goodale's 2005 budget (his final one, as it turned out). At the time, an official with the Department of Finance told me that after a meeting between senior officials and unnamed experts, it had been decided to shelve the program and simply raise RRSP contribution limits instead.

The reasons for abandoning the concept at that time were never clearly spelled out. However, those familiar with the discussions believe that officials in Finance were concerned about two issues: the cost of such a program over time and the potential political fallout when Guaranteed Income Supplement (GIS) recipients with RRSPs or Registered Retirement Income Funds (RRIFs) caught on to the fact that their benefits were being clawed back as they drew out money while people with TFSAs were not being similarly penalized. As well, there had been growing complaints over the years about the complexity of the tax system, and introducing TFSAs would add another dimension to that problem.

Another factor was the absence of any strong voter constituency to support the idea. The social rationale for the TFSA concept is that it will be of the greatest benefit to people with modest incomes. But they don't have the kind of political clout that, for example, farmers and manufacturers do.

So the TPSP concept remained in limbo for four years, until Jim Flaherty suddenly, and unexpectedly, resurrected it as TFSA in the 2008 budget.

As I noted in Chapter 1, there had been no hint it was coming. Pre-budget speculation took a "cupboard is bare" stance, noting that the finance minister had trotted out all his goodies in the previous fall's Economic Statement, which at the time was expected to kick off an election campaign. However, the opposition parties refused to co-operate with that scheme by defeating the Conservatives in the House of Commons, leaving Flaherty with nothing more to give.

The minister went out of his way to dampen budget expectations, saying in advance that he was not going to "throw money around" or put the country back into deficit by cutting taxes further.

"The fiscal chickens have come home, and are roosting uneasily on Jim Flaherty's shoulders," *The Globe and Mail* commented in a pre-budget editorial. "His options are far narrower now. His leeway is lost. The GST was the wrong tax to cut, at the wrong time. Now Mr. Flaherty has to pinch pennies."[2]

Faced with the prospect of a ho-hum budget in what would likely be an election year (and was, as it turned out), the finance minister and his staff started casting around for ideas. In pre-budget consultations with a range of business people, academics, and special interest groups, Finance officials kept returning to two key themes: demographics and retirement. As a subtext, the minister was very aware of the lingering anger among many seniors over his decision to impose a tax on income trusts, which was announced October 31, 2006.

In its "shadow budget" brief to the government prior to the 2008 budget, the C.D. Howe Institute returned to the theme of Tax-Free Savings Accounts, which it had been promoting since 2001 (more on that in a moment). However, it rated only six lines in a 13-page report—it was almost as if the institute had given up.[3]

Whether it was that reference or something else that was the trigger, the minister seized on the idea. It was a good ideological fit:

The concept had been part of his party's 2004 campaign platform (a campaign the Tories lost to Paul Martin's Liberals). On page 16 of the platform, a one-line sentence in the tax section had made this promise: "Introduce a new Registered Lifetime Savings Plan that will allow Canadians to withdraw their money tax-free."[4]

Interestingly, the concept was not restated in the 2006 platform, *Stand Up for Canada*. Instead, the Tories promised a much more sweeping overhaul of investment policy, saying they would "eliminate the capital gains tax for individuals on the sale of assets when the proceeds are reinvested within six months." Expanding on this, the platform went on: "Canadians who invest, or inherit cottages or family heirlooms, should be able to sell those assets and plough their profits back into the economy without taking a tax hit. It is time government rewarded Canadians who reinvest their money and create jobs." When I visited the official website of the Conservative Party in September 2008, while the election campaign was on, the 2006 platform had been expunged. A Google search enabled me to retrieve it from www.scribd.com.[5]

The 2004 campaign promise was clearly based on the same concept that Goodale had mused about in the 2003 and 2004 budgets, which is perhaps why the Conservatives chose to abandon it in 2006. But by early winter 2008, things were looking desperate, and Flaherty needed a showcase idea that wouldn't cost much but that would have broad appeal and look good in the media headlines. The TFSA concept fit the bill—especially the negligible initial cost. It also had the added attraction of addressing the 2006 capital gains promise, albeit on a much-scaled-back basis. The minister had his officials massage it into a comprehensive plan and took it to Prime Minister Harper, who micro-manages everything in Ottawa these days. Once Harper signed on, Cabinet approval was virtually a rubber stamp. Months later, during the 2008 election campaign,

Harper described TFSAs as "our first cut" at capital gains tax reform during an interview with Amanda Lang, who was then with the Business News Network.

So both the Liberals and the Conservatives looked at the TFSA concept between 2003 and 2005, although it was never presented as a high priority. But where did the original idea come from?

The British Model

Britain created a similar program over a decade ago, in April 1999. The Individual Savings Account (ISA) has become quite popular. According to a report written by CIBC senior economist Benjamin Tal in September 2008, 37 percent of British citizens have opened ISAs, contributing an average of £2500 a year (the maximum allowed is £7200). Tal said the number of new accounts is increasing at an annual rate of 6 percent and that ISAs have become a £270 billion market in the United Kingdom.[6]

The Canadian TFSA concept is closely modelled on the British program but offers more flexibility to investors. The British plan gives people two options. One is called a cash ISA, the other a stocks and shares ISA.[7] These must be separate plans and cannot be combined, making them more awkward than a TFSA, which can include all types of securities, depending on the type of plan chosen. Effective April 2010, all U.K. residents can invest up to £10,200 annually in their plans.

Using an exchange rate of £1 equals CDN$1.75, this means U.K. residents can contribute the equivalent of CDN$17,850 a year to an ISA, more than three and a half times the initial contribution limit in this country.[8]

The Roth IRA

In the United States, the closest thing to the ISA or the TFSA is the Roth Individual Retirement Account (Roth IRA). It actually pre-dates the ISA, having been created in 1998, but it is nowhere near as attractive a savings vehicle as the other two.

As with the British and Canadian plans, contributions to a Roth IRA are not tax-deductible. Unlike the others, however, the maximum annual amount that can be contributed is determined by age. In 2009, Americans under age 50 were allowed to contribute a maximum of $5000 a year, while older citizens could contribute up to $6000. (These figures will be adjusted for inflation in 2010.) Income earned by investments in a Roth IRA are tax-sheltered but can only be withdrawn from the plan tax-free after a holding period of five years or when the investor reaches the age of 59 and six months. There are also income limits for contribution eligibility. None of these constraints apply to the Canadian plan.

The Role of the C.D. Howe Institute

The leading advocate for the introduction of Tax-Free Savings Accounts in Canada was the C.D. Howe Institute, a non-partisan think-tank based in Toronto that has been an influential voice in public policy since 1958. (C.D. Howe was a senior Liberal Cabinet minister who served in Parliament for 22 years.)

The institute began advocating what it called Tax-Prepaid Savings Plans (TPSPs) as early as February 2001, in a study titled *A New Option for Retirement Savings: Tax-Prepaid Savings Plans*. Authors Jonathan Kesselman, an economics professor at the University of British Columbia, and Finn Poschmann, now director of research at the C.D. Howe Institute, argued that the existing retirement savings system did not work well for lower-income people and increased the likelihood that they would need support from the public purse in their later years. The document attracted little media interest.

In 2003, the institute raised the ante with the publication of a scathing attack on the unfairness of existing savings plans as they relate to low-income Canadians. The paper was titled *New Poverty Traps: Means Testing and Modest-Income Seniors.*[9] The author, Richard Shillington, holds a doctoral degree in statistics and has been carrying out research into health, social, and economic policies for more than 30 years. His analysis raised serious issues relating to how lower-income seniors who have saved for their retirement are penalized by the way in which government support programs are administered.

Shillington did not mince words. Millions of people who are at or approaching retirement age "are victims of a fraud, however unintentional," he wrote. Saving through RRSPs was likely to make them poorer in retirement, not better off, because most of their RRSP income "will be confiscated by income-tested programs and income taxes."

Government policy-makers were urged to take a close look at the situation and to introduce policies to deal with it as quickly as possible. Specifically, Shillington advocated the creation of TPSPs, similar to the British ISA or the Roth IRA in the United States, which, he said, would meet the retirement savings needs of lower-income Canadians more effectively.

The Liberal government of the day didn't act, so in November 2004, the institute launched yet another initiative. Finn Poschmann and then–senior vice-president and director of research (now CEO) William B.P. Robson co-authored another detailed backgrounder on the topic.

Titled *Saving's Grace: A Framework to Promote Financial Independence for Low-Income Canadians*, the report criticized the federal government for creating a range of savings plans for retirement and education that were better suited to the needs of middle- and upper-income people.[10] Plans such as RRSPs and Registered Pension Plans (RPPs) are not useful for lower-income Canadians, they argued, because the tax savings they offer are negligible (RRSP contributions are treated as deductions, which means the higher a person's bracket, the greater the tax savings). When the money is needed, any withdrawals are taxed, perhaps at a higher rate than the value of the original deduction. Plus, any pension or RRIF payments or RRSP withdrawals reduce eligibility for a range of government benefits, such as the Guaranteed Income Supplement, and government tax credits.

The report urged the federal government to create a new, broadly based, easy-to-understand savings program that would be available to all Canadians, regardless of income. The plan should have as few restrictions as possible, offer generous carry-forward provisions, and allow tax-free withdrawals at any time. Especially important, withdrawals should not be considered as income for means-tested programs, subsidies, and tax credits.

The authors concluded by calling the case for such a plan "compelling." In particular, they said that, TPSPs would "let many low-income earners escape the punitive treatment they now suffer at the hands of federal and provincial taxes and benefit claw-backs."

Reading the document today, it seems to have been the blueprint used by the Conservatives for the plan introduced in the 2008 budget, right down to the smallest detail. Not surprisingly, Robson and his colleagues were elated. "It was a worthy centrepiece for a budget," he told me. "This is a revolutionary type of savings vehicle for Canada."

Jim Flaherty acknowledged the role the institute played in bringing TFSAs to reality when he visited its headquarters a few days after his budget was unveiled. A framed, autographed copy of his Budget Speech now hangs on the wall in Poschmann's office.

The Next Steps

But the story isn't over yet. There are still some roadblocks to overcome if TFSAs are going to function at maximum efficiency.

Canada has a patchwork quilt of social-assistance programs, with conditions and restrictions that vary greatly from one province to another. William Robson described the net effect as "fiendishly complicated and fantastically un-coordinated."

Unless provincial and territorial laws are changed, social programs that apply means tests and/or asset tests to determine eligibility will discourage lower-income people from using TFSAs to save money.

A brief published on September 30, 2008, by the C.D. Howe Institute said that saving money will be "pointless" for anyone who faces clawbacks of social benefits for doing so.[11]

"Having modest savings (as low as $560 in Ontario for a single welfare recipient) can make one ineligible for support programs, like social assistance, which include asset tests," said the brief's authors, John Stapleton and Richard Shillington. "When governments penalize beneficiaries for saving, by reducing program benefits, these programs become traps."

The brief called on the provinces and territories to pass legislation to ensure that TFSAs work properly. This would be achieved by specifying a level up to which people could accumulate TFSA savings without losing benefits, by defining to whom the ceiling will apply (current recipients, new applicants, or both), and by clarifying the conditions under which people can make TFSA withdrawals without jeopardizing social benefits.

The institute also recommended that governments consider building on the TFSA platform by supplementing the savings of lower-income people. The Canada Education Savings Grant, which is added to Registered Education Savings Plan (RESP) contributions, was cited as an example.

A year later, there had been little movement on this issue.

So there may be more chapters to come in the TFSA story. But everyone seems to agree that what we now have in place is a valuable first step.

3

The Basic Rules

Once people understand the concept of TFSAs, they quickly embrace the idea. A Scotiabank survey carried out a few months after the 2008 budget announcement found that although awareness was still low at the time, Canadians reacted enthusiastically when the key points of the program were explained.

"Most Canadians single out the tax savings as most appealing, although many also find the flexibility to withdraw funds without compromising contribution room compelling," the survey analysis concluded. "Overall, most Canadians (60%) view the TFSA as an 'ideal savings and investment account' for them."[1]

As it turned out, the Scotiabank findings were accurate. Canadians began opening accounts even before the official launch date after several financial institutions started aggressively promoting the plans in the fall of 2008. Less than two months after ING DIRECT Canada began offering TFSAs in October of that year, the president of the company, Peter Aceto, reported that 170,000 accounts had been opened. "We've actually been a bit surprised by the overwhelming response," he said.

Despite the initial enthusiasm, it soon became apparent that many people had little understanding of the rules governing

TFSAs. And based on the questions I received all through 2009, that is still the case.

So, before we get into the strategies for making TFSAs work most effectively for you, let's review the key points you need to know about these plans and how they differ from RRSPs and RESPs.

Eligibility. You must be a resident of Canada to open a TFSA. You have to provide your Social Insurance Number (SIN) and date of birth when you set up a plan.

Age limit. In theory, anyone 18 or older can open a TFSA. That's what the federal legislation says. However, sometimes things are not always simple in Canada because of conflicting federal and provincial jurisdictions. This is one of those cases.

In some provinces and territories, the age of majority is 19 (British Columbia, New Brunswick, Newfoundland and Labrador, Northwest Territories, Nova Scotia, Nunavut, and Yukon). This means that contracts entered into by 18-year-olds, who are legally minors in those jurisdictions, can be voided by the courts if challenged.

"This issue is directly related to risk management and is not based on a firm rule per se," says Jason Enouy, senior manager, Process & Regulatory Solutions, Scotiabank Wealth Management. "At law, and generally speaking, contracts entered into by minors are *voidable* if challenged in court. Importantly, however, they are not *void* automatically (or *ab initio*). This means that where a minor opens a TFSA, her account agreement and investment directions are legitimate and in force until they are successfully challenged. Since the federal government has set the minimum age for TFSAs as 18, anyone in Canada may open one at that age.

However, as the age of majority is 19 in some provinces, there exists a disparity between federal and provincial law (as is often the case). A quick shorthand is that the federal government is concerned with taxation, while the provinces are concerned with property (including contracts), which results in different age considerations."

As a result, there are differing rules on the minimum age for starting a TFSA depending on which financial institution you deal with. For example, Scotiabank allows 18-year-olds to open plans that invest only in savings accounts and GICs. However, subsidiaries such as brokerage firm ScotiaMcLeod require clients to have reached the age of majority in these cases before they will open a TFSA that can invest in stocks, mutual funds, and so on. If you live in one of the affected provinces/territories and have an 18-year-old family member who wants to set up a TFSA, ask your financial institution about its policy on age.

In all cases, accumulation of contribution room will start at 18 even if a plan cannot be opened for another year.

There is no maximum age for holding a TFSA. This differs in two important ways from RRSPs. Although most people don't realize it, even a child can open an RRSP as long as he or she has earned income. If your baby girl is chosen to star in a television commercial, the income she earns could be used to open an RRSP. That's not the case with TFSAs—only adults need apply.

At the other end of the age scale, the government does not allow you to hold an RRSP past December 31 of the year in which you turn 71. At that time, you must cash in the plan, convert it to a RRIF, or buy an annuity. That leaves older Canadians without a simple and cheap tax shelter and, as the population ages, more people are becoming concerned about that.

TFSAs are the answer. Since there is no termination date for these plans, you can keep contributing to them (thereby sheltering investment income) until the day you die.

Contribution limit. The initial contribution limit was set at $5000 per person and that maximum applies for 2010. The limit is indexed to inflation and, theoretically at least, adjusted annually. But there is some small print in the regulations that makes it unlikely there will be any change in the maximum for another few years. There will also probably be several years between subsequent increases.

The Department of Finance decided to move away from the standard annual indexing formula that is used for tax brackets, CPP payments, tax credits, and so forth. Instead, Finance introduced a new type of indexing, which, it says, provides "simplification and certainty." (It will also slow the drain that TFSAs will have on the public purse, but Finance officials say that was not a major factor in the decision.) The TFSA formula requires that indexing be done in increments of $500. This means the limit will be rounded up or down each year. The effect will be to delay the first increase in the TFSA contribution limit until the inflation factor has reached at least $250. Assuming an average annual inflation rate of 2 percent, the following chart indicates what we can expect in changes to the maximum contribution limit over the next few years.

As you can see, the first increase in the annual maximum contribution will not occur until 2012 unless inflation runs at a higher rate than the Bank of Canada target. It will be 2017 before the limit moves up again, to $6000, and 2021 before we reach $6500.

To put this into perspective, the maximum allowable RRSP contribution for 2010 is $22,000. It will take decades for TFSAs to

Projected TFSA Contribution Limits

Year	Cumulative inflation factor*	Contribution limit
2010	$5100	$5000
2011	$5202	$5000
2012	$5306	$5500
2013	$5412	$5500
2014	$5520	$5500
2015	$5631	$5500
2016	$5743	$5500
2017	$5858	$6000
2018	$5975	$6000
2019	$6095	$6000
2020	$6217	$6000
2021	$6341	$6500

* Assumes annual inflation rate of 2%.

come anywhere near that. This will become an important consideration when we examine TFSAs versus RRSPs as retirement savings options in Chapter 6.

Contributions in kind. You don't need to have cash to make a TFSA contribution. You can also build a plan through what are known as contributions in kind. This allows you to deposit securities you already own directly to a TFSA. For example, suppose you have $4500 invested in a guaranteed investment certificate (GIC) that does not mature for three years. You can start tax-sheltering the interest immediately by contributing to your plan. You have to pay tax on the interest you earn up to the time you contributed it to your TFSA, but after that, all your profit is tax-free. However, there is a potential trap here. If the total value of the GIC (principal plus accrued interest) exceeds $5000, you run the risk of an overcontribution. Before you issue instructions, check the current value of the certificate and make sure you have enough contribution room to accommodate it.

The rules governing TFSA contributions are the same as those for RRSPs, so there are a couple of points you need to consider before making use of this strategy.

First, if you make a contribution in kind, the Canada Revenue Agency treats the transaction as if you sold the security on the day it went into the plan. This means that if you have a capital gain, for example on a stock or mutual fund, that gain is triggered when you make the contribution and must be declared on your income tax return for that year.

The second point to remember is that, while you will have to pay tax on any capital gains created by contributing a security to a TFSA, you may not claim a capital loss. This distortion in the tax rules has burned some people who decided to dump losing stocks into their RRSPs only to discover too late that the loss was not tax-deductible.

So never contribute a money-losing security directly to a TFSA. Sell it first, thereby creating a deductible capital loss, and then put the cash from the sale into the plan.

Swaps. Swaps involve exchanging cash or securities from outside a TFSA for assets of equal value inside the plan. For example, you may wish to put $5000 worth of new cash into your TFSA and withdraw $5000 worth of mutual fund units simultaneously. Initially, the Department of Finance said swaps would not be allowed because the assets coming out of the plan would represent a withdrawal and therefore would not create new contribution room until the following year.

However, in January 2009, the Canada Revenue Agency adopted a more liberal stance, saying TFSA swaps would be treated in the same way as RRSP swaps. The CRA has responsibility for interpreting the tax laws, so as a result of its position, TFSA swaps are legal.

In October 2009, after receiving evidence that some people were aggressively using swaps to dramatically increase the value of their TFSAs, Finance announced proposed changes to the Income Tax Act that will prohibit such transactions in future from either non-registered or registered accounts (such as RRSPs). So swaps are once again off limits.

Overcontributions. Avoid making any overcontributions. The penalties are draconian. In October 2009, the Finance Department announced that any profits from intentional overcontributions will be taxed at a rate of 100 percent! If you make an overcontribution by mistake, withdraw the money from the plan as soon as you discover the error. Unlike with RRSPs, there is no $2000 lifetime overcontribution allowed.

Deductions. There are none. You do not receive any tax relief for a TFSA contribution. Any money that goes into a plan is on an after-tax basis (RESPs operate the same way). This is a major difference between TFSAs and RRSPs—one that will certainly cause a lot of head-scratching as people decide which plan they should contribute to.

Carry-forwards. The rules are similar to those for RRSPs in that any unused contribution room may be carried forward indefinitely.

For example, if you contributed only $2000 to a new TFSA in 2009, your limit in 2010 is $8000 ($5000 plus the $3000 carried forward from 2009).

You do not have to file a tax return to accumulate carry-forward room. However, if you don't do so, the Canada Revenue Agency will not be able to keep track of the amount you are allowed to put into a TFSA. You will need to do that yourself.

TFSA year-end. For purposes of contributions and carry-forwards, TFSAs operate on a calendar-year basis, so the annual cut-off date is December 31. This means TFSAs use the same clock as RESPs. (RRSP contributions, by contrast, may be made up to 60 days after the end of the calendar year.)

Number of plans. As with RRSPs, there is no limit on the number of TFSAs you can open. But common sense suggests that you limit yourself to one plan for ease of administration. If you decide to open a second TFSA, make sure you have a good reason for doing so.

Withdrawals. You can take money out of a TFSA at any time, with no tax consequences. You don't even have to declare it on your income tax return—it is like withdrawing money from your bank savings account. And here is an interesting twist: Unlike with RRSPs, any amount you withdraw is added back to your contribution limit for the next year. (Exceptions include withdrawals relating to overcontributions, prohibited or non-qualifying investments, asset transfers, and any profits derived from these sources.)

Let's suppose you accumulate $20,000 in a TFSA between now and 2013. At that point, you decide to draw out $15,000 to help pay for a new car. Assuming that the annual contribution limit at that time is $5500, your personal limit for 2014 will be $20,500—

the basic maximum plus the amount you took out of the plan for the car purchase.

Note that you cannot recontribute withdrawn amounts within the same calendar year. You must wait until January 1 of the year following. So if you withdraw $2000 in 2010, that amount does not become part of your legal contribution room until 2011.

Taxes. Although you don't get a tax deduction when you contribute, all withdrawals from your TFSA are tax-free. The investment income earned within the plan is fully sheltered, forever—unlike RRSPs, where all investment income earned within a plan is taxed at your marginal taxation rate when you withdraw it. TFSAs thus provide a way to earn investment income without incurring any tax liability, now or in the future.

Reporting. Although TFSAs aren't taxable, the Canada Revenue Agency will need to keep tabs on your plan in order to determine how much you are allowed to contribute in any given year. The reporting responsibility is in the hands of the financial institution that administers your plan, which files an annual information return. This includes details of all contributions, withdrawals, and transfers made during the year as well as the value of the plan's assets at the beginning and end of the year. Your annual income tax notice of assessment will contain a section advising you of the status of your TFSA—in the same way as your RRSP contribution room is currently shown.

Income testing. TFSA withdrawals are not considered as income. So they don't compromise your eligibility for income-tested tax credits such as the Age Credit, the Canada Child Tax Benefit, the Working Income Tax Benefit, or the GST tax credit. You can withdraw money from TFSAs without affecting Employment Insurance benefits. For older Canadians, TFSA withdrawals don't affect their eligibility for programs such as the Guaranteed Income Supplement (GIS) and don't result in Old Age Security (OAS) clawbacks.

This is very important for lower-income seniors. Under current rules, GIS payments are cut by 50 cents for every $1 worth of income a recipient receives, including the income from RRSP withdrawals and RRIF payments. So low-income seniors receiving GIS see their payments eroded because they made the effort to save a little for retirement. That's why, in his 2003 paper, Dr. Richard Shillington[2] of the C.D. Howe Institute suggested that people who expect to qualify for GIS should not make RRSP contributions and advised the government to introduce a TFSA-like program instead. It took six years, but it finally happened.

Investments. TFSAs are highly flexible when it comes to the investments you can choose. The rules for qualified securities are the same as those applied to RRSPs. Almost anything is allowed: guaranteed investment certificates, mutual funds, stocks (Canadian and foreign), bonds, gold, and cash. Even shares in a small business are eligible under certain conditions (see Chapter 12 for more details). The major exceptions (as with RRSPs) are real estate and non-arm's-length investments. If you are uncertain whether an investment qualifies, get professional advice before going ahead, because the penalties for including non-eligible investments in a TFSA can be severe. In October 2009, the Department of Finance announced amendments to the Income Tax Act that will impose a 100-percent tax on any income attributed to non-qualified investments held in a TFSA.

Deposit insurance. Certain types of TFSA deposits are covered up to $100,000 by the Canada Deposit Insurance Corporation (CDIC), including cash, term deposits, and guaranteed investment certificates. But as a general rule, most securities, including stocks and mutual funds, are not covered. That includes money market funds. For complete details on federal deposit insurance, visit www.cdic.ca.

Interest deductibility. You may borrow money to invest in a TFSA, but you cannot claim the interest on the loan as a tax deduction. These rules are the same as for RRSPs.

Spousal plans. Unlike RRSPs, there are no spousal TFSAs. Also, there is no such thing as a joint TFSA—each plan is the property of one individual. However, one spouse is permitted to give the other the money to open a TFSA. See "Income splitting" for more details.

Income splitting. The usual income-attribution rules do not apply to TFSAs. This means one spouse can provide the money for the other to open an account without penalty. So, even if the other spouse has no income or savings, he or she can have a TFSA. Over the years, this could lead to big tax savings for families. See Chapter 9 for more information.

Marriage breakdown. TFSA assets can be transferred from the plan of one spouse or partner to the plan of the other in the event of a marriage breakdown. However, in this case, the person from whom the money is transferred is not given new contribution room to compensate, as this is not considered to be a withdrawal. Any such transfer does not count against the contribution room of the spouse or partner who receives the money.

Transfers. You can transfer assets from one of your own TFSAs to another one. This is called a "qualifying transfer." If you want to move the money into an RRSP, you can make a tax-free withdrawal from the TFSA and contribute directly to the RRSP, which will generate a tax deduction. However, and this question has been asked of me a lot, you cannot transfer money from an RRSP to a TFSA. Many people thought that would be a great idea because it would avoid the tax on RRSP withdrawals. Sadly, it's a non-starter.

Loan collateral. Unlike RRSPs, a TFSA can be used as collateral for loans. This could be useful in a situation where you suddenly need cash to deal with an emergency, but the money in your TFSA is not accessible, perhaps because it has been invested in a locked-in GIC. If the lender is satisfied that the assets in the plan are sound, the TFSA can serve as collateral for a cash advance.

There is one important exception. In order to prevent TFSA contribution room from being "sold" or "rented," any loan agreement must be on an arm's-length basis. If the propriety of a loan is questioned, you'll have to be able to show that the loan was not intended to "enable another person or partnership to benefit from the exemption from tax" provided by the TFSA exemption.

Living abroad. If you leave Canada after opening a TFSA, you can maintain the account and continue to make withdrawals. However, you will have to check whether such withdrawals would be regarded as tax-free by the country in which you are residing. You may not make any new contributions while you are out of the country and no new contribution room will accrue. If you contribute to a TFSA while you are a non-resident, you will be assessed a penalty tax of 1 percent a month until the amount is withdrawn or you become a legal resident again.

(Note: It is possible to be a Canadian resident even if you live outside the country, as long as you have close ties with Canada. This might include having a home and personal property in the country, a spouse or dependants in Canada, being eligible for provincial medical insurance, and so on. More details can be found in the Canada Revenue Agency's Interpretation Bulletin IT-221R.)

Plan termination. A TFSA ceases to exist when the last account holder dies, the plan ceases to qualify for whatever reason, or the account is not being administered according to the law.

Death. When you die, the assets in your TFSA can be transferred to the plan of your spouse or common-law partner if he or she is named as your sole beneficiary in the TFSA contract. In that case, he/she becomes the successor account holder. Things get more complicated when the last spouse or partner dies, but essentially all of the assets in a TFSA at the time of death can pass to the next generation tax-free. More details are presented in Chapter 10.

4

The "Magic" of TFSAs

Quick now, what is often referred to as the "eighth wonder of the world"?

The answer is compound interest. It's a simple but powerful way to get rich, provided you have time and a little self-discipline.

Before we go any further, let me clarify an important point. Although the term generally used is *compound interest*, what we are really talking about is compounded profits from investment income of any kind. That can include dividends, rental income, capital gains, and anything else you earn from your invested money. So for the purposes of this discussion, I'll use the all-encompassing term of *compound income*.

Compound income simply amounts to profit earning more profit. If you invest $1 at 4 percent, after one year you'll have $1.04. Now you'll start to earn income on that extra four cents as well as on your original dollar. It doesn't happen quickly, but over the years, that can add up to a lot of money.

The Rule of 72 is a classic way to calculate how long it will take for an amount of money to double in value through compounding. To use it, simply divide the return on the invested money by 72. For instance, if you invest $1000 at an annual rate of return of

4 percent, it will take 18 years for your money to double (72 ÷ 4). But if your money earns 6 percent, it will double in only 12 years (72 ÷ 6).

Of course, this assumes that you get to keep all the investment income for yourself. In reality, the government keeps dipping its sticky fingers into your profits. And that's been the big problem for Canadians until now. We've had no way to fully benefit from the magic of compound income in this country because Ottawa and the provinces are always taking a share of the pie.

You may ask, What about RRSPs? While it's true that any investment income that is earned in retirement savings plans is tax-sheltered, you're hit with a big tax bite when you take the money out.

For example, suppose you contribute $1000 a year to an RRSP over 30 years and invest the money in guaranteed investment certificates that pay an average annual return of 5 percent. At the end of that time, the plan is valued at $69,761. Subtracting your $30,000 in contributions, you have earned investment income totalling almost $40,000.

But as soon as you start taking money out of that RRSP, the government swoops in and taxes it. If you are in the 30-percent bracket, you'll give back $12,000 of the income you've earned over all those years to the tax folks. You get to keep only $28,000 for yourself. The 5 percent you thought you earned ended up only being about 4 percent in after-tax terms. If you are in a 40-percent bracket, your after-tax profit drops to $24,000. Suddenly, compounding doesn't seem quite so magical any more.

Tax-Free Savings Accounts change everything. For the first time, we have access to an investment vehicle that allows us to obtain the full benefit of compounding. The income we earn in a TFSA is 100 percent ours to keep. No part of it will be taxed away.

Here's a table that illustrates what this means in terms of wealth building over time and shows the value of the TFSA at the end of various time frames. I've assumed an average annual compound rate of return of 5 percent in all cases.

TFSA Growth at 5 Percent

Annual contribution	10 years	20 years	30 years	40 years
$1000	$13,207	$34,719	$69,761	$126,840
$2000	$26,414	$69,439	$139,522	$253,680
$3000	$39,620	$104,158	$209,282	$380,519
$4000	$52,827	$138,877	$279,043	$507,359
$5000	$66,034	$173,596	$348,804	$634,199

Assumption: Contribution is made at start of year.

In case you're wondering, it would take 50 years for the value of the plan to surpass $1 million based on an annual contribution of $5000. With life expectancy increasing, readers who are 25 today have a realistic hope of achieving that $1 million. Also, remember that couples can save twice as much. We'll examine the implications of that in Chapter 12.

Take a close look at the numbers in this table. There are two key points to take away.

Start young. Compounding is like a rolling snowball. It takes time to gather speed and mass. The more years a plan has to grow, the more impressive the returns will be.

Look at the $1000 line in the table. After one decade, the plan has only added $3207 to your original $10,000 in contributions.

But after 20 years, the investment income earned within the plan has ballooned to $14,719 ($34,719 minus $20,000 in contributions). After 40 years, the magic of compounding has given you a total, tax-free profit of $86,840!

So, the sooner you begin, the more effectively a TFSA can work for you. Obviously, none of us can turn back time. But however old you are today, the same basic rule applies: The sooner you begin, the more effective a TFSA will be.

Contribute as much as you can. Slide your eyes down each column. You'll see that the more money you contribute annually, the more profitable a TFSA becomes over the years. If you double the annual contribution from $1000 to $2000, your profit from compounding also doubles after the first decade, from $3207 to $6414. If you are able to contribute the initial maximum amount of $5000 annually, your 10-year profit increases to $16,034. (Of course, these figures assume no withdrawals are made along the way.)

The powerhouse effect of combining high contributions with many years of growth is apparent in the cell on the bottom right of the table. This shows you how much money is in a plan after 40 years of growth at 5 percent with an annual contribution of $5000. The total is $634,199, which means your tax-free profit after deducting all contributions is $434,199. That's a nice nest egg to draw on in retirement!

An Extra Point of Return

Now let's play with these numbers a little. The next table shows you the value of a TFSA if you are able to add one percentage point of annual return over the years, moving from 5 percent to 6 percent.

TFSA Growth at 6 Percent

Annual contribution	10 years	20 years	30 years	40 years
$1000	$13,972	$38,993	$83,802	$164,048
$2000	$27,943	$77,985	$167,603	$328,095
$3000	$41,915	$116,978	$251,405	$492,143
$4000	$55,887	$155,971	$335,207	$656,191
$5000	$69,858	$194,964	$419,008	$820,238

Assumption: Contribution is made at start of year.

What a difference a percentage point makes over time! After a decade, that extra return doesn't translate into a large profit gain—at the $1000 annual contribution level, the additional growth is only $765, which suggests that for older people the added risk involved may not be worth it. But look what happens as the years pass and the magic of compounding takes hold. Staying with the $1000 contributor, at the end of the second decade the additional gain is $4274. After 40 years, this person is ahead by $37,208 because he or she invested the money wisely and earned one percentage point more.

Here again, the more you contribute, the greater the impact of the extra percentage point of return. An annual contribution of $5000 that is invested to earn an average annual gain of 5 percent grows to $634,199 after 40 years. But at 6 percent, the TFSA is worth $820,238 at that stage. The extra percentage point has given you an additional $186,039 to help fund your retirement. Now that's impressive!

End-of-Year Contributions

Finally, let's look at one more set of numbers. The tables we've looked at so far assume that TFSA contributions are made at the start of each calendar year, on January 1. Most people, however, tend to put things off. So let's see what happens if the contributions are delayed to the last minute, to December 31 of the same year. Here's what our 6-percent table would look like in those circumstances.

TFSA Growth at 6 Percent

Annual contribution	10 years	20 years	30 years	40 years
$1000	$13,181	$36,786	$79,058	$154,762
$2000	$26,362	$73,571	$158,116	$309,524
$3000	$39,542	$110,357	$237,175	$464,286
$4000	$52,723	$147,142	$316,233	$619,048
$5000	$65,904	$183,928	$395,291	$773,804

Assumption: Contribution is made at end of year.

This may be difficult to believe, but waiting until the end of each year to make a TFSA contribution can end up costing you tens of thousands of dollars in lost profit (the same applies to RRSPs, by the way). Again, you don't notice much of an impact in the early years, but as the compounding snowball begins to gain momentum, the price of delaying starts to add up.

The person who contributes $3000 annually on December 31 of each year has $6621 less profit after 20 years than someone who makes the same contribution 12 months earlier, on January 1.

As we move out to 40 years, the impact of delaying a contribution really hits hard. Someone who puts $5000 a year into a TFSA on January 1 of each year over that time will have a plan worth $820,238. The person who waits until year-end will have only $773,804. That's a difference of more than $46,000, proving once again that procrastination can be expensive.

Action Summary

1. Start immediately. Set up a TFSA as soon as you can. The more years your money can grow tax-sheltered, the wealthier you will be.
2. Contribute as much as possible. Any amount is better than nothing, but if you stretch a little, the reward at the end will be much greater.
3. Contribute early. Don't wait until New Year's Eve to make your annual contribution. Get the money into the plan as early in the year as possible.
4. Within reason, aim for a higher return. Don't take needless risks with your TFSA money, but don't be overly conservative either, especially if you are under 50. An extra percentage point of profit will add thousands of dollars to your wealth over the years.

5

Rainy Day TFSAs

Every financial expert will tell you the same thing: All families should have an emergency cash reserve to help them get through difficult times. The problem is that in recent years few people have been paying attention to this basic rule of money management. The idea of putting something aside for a rainy day didn't resonate when the sun was shining all the time. However, the deep recession of 2008–2009 made saving for the future a higher priority for many families.

Although it took an economic crisis to force a change in attitude, the long-term result could be positive. In the United States, the savings rate had fallen to close to zero and was threatening to slip into negative territory, a phenomenon unheard of since the Great Depression of the 1930s. Canadians had also succumbed to the same virus, with Statistics Canada reporting that at the end of June 2008, the average household was carrying a debt load of $1.25 for every $1 of personal disposable income.[1]

The sub-prime mortgage disaster in the United States was a chilling lesson in just how destructive too much debt can be. Americans lost their homes to foreclosures at a higher rate than at any time since the 1930s. Thousands of decent people ended up on the street because they could not meet their mortgage payments. Had they put some money into an emergency savings account over the years, they might have been able to survive.

I believe that we are going to see more emphasis on saving in the next few years as a result of people realizing the danger of over-extending themselves. As it happens, the fortuitous timing of the introduction of Tax-Free Savings Accounts makes saving easier and more financially attractive.

Until now, there has not been any truly effective way to build an emergency fund. Putting the money in a regular bank savings account is easy and safe, but it pays no return to speak of. In fact, when inflation and taxes are factored in, your emergency fund probably loses some value each year.

A high-interest savings account is a better choice, but unless it is inside a TFSA the return on your savings will still be negligible after taxes and inflation are calculated. For example, suppose you put $1000 of emergency money into a high-interest savings account that pays 3 percent a year. You are in the 30-percent tax bracket, and the inflation rate is 2 percent. Your statement shows that you earn $30 a year on your money. But the government grabs $9 of that in taxes, and inflation reduces the buying power of your savings by $20, to $980. Your real return on your savings for that year is only $1! That works out to 0.1 percent. "Why bother?" you may ask.

Some people have tried to get around this dilemma by using their RRSPs as an emergency fund; it's an approach I suggested in my book *Get Control of Your Money*, which was published in 2003. The RRSP strategy offers the advantage of an immediate tax refund and postpones the tax bite on investment income until the money is withdrawn. But the downside is that this approach could actually end up costing you more in the end. That's because you may have to withdraw cash for an emergency at a time when you are in a higher tax bracket than you were when you originally contributed the money. Also, a withholding tax of anywhere from 10 percent to 30 percent applies to all RRSP withdrawals except in Quebec, where the minimum is 21 percent and the maximum 35 percent. Although you'll get credit for any tax withheld when you file your annual tax return, it means you won't have access to all your money at a time when you may need it most.

The ideal emergency fund allows you quick access to your cash whenever you need it while providing tax-sheltering for the income your money earns in the meantime. That's the precise description of a TFSA. These plans are the perfect vehicles for building your emergency savings account, which means that every family should have one.

If you already have an emergency fund, your first step should be to open a TFSA (and one for your spouse or partner as well) and move the money into the plan. If you have not created such a fund, now is the ideal time to start. It should be the first priority in building your TFSA.

Gillian Riley, Scotiabank's managing director and head of retail deposits, puts it this way: "When thinking about the TFSA and how Canadians can apply it to their personal financial situation, I would recommend that they look at how they use their traditional savings account and consider using the TFSA instead to earn tax-free growth. The TFSA is a tool that should inspire Canadians to save because of its added benefits and versatility."

Of course, the best time to build an emergency fund is when your budget is under control and you can free up some cash. The problem is that people always find something on which to spend any extra money they earn. When budgets are stretched, saving becomes even harder. Sure, an emergency fund may be a fine idea.

But after paying the household bills, the mortgage, the car loan, the dentist, and all the other bills, there's nothing left over.

So you must make building your emergency fund a priority. You have to decide that this is a financial cushion your family simply must have and that one way or another you're going to make it happen, even if it means some sacrifices. That's why it needs to be included as an integral part of the family budget. Commitment is half the battle.

How Big a Fund?

Generally, I recommend your emergency fund be equal to at least three months' worth of family take-home pay (after tax). Some experts counsel having a six-month reserve, and I have recently seen some popular U.S. financial gurus suggesting that eight months' worth of income be set aside.

To put this in dollar terms, let's look at the case of a childless couple, with each person earning taxable income of $60,000. So the total family taxable income is $120,000 a year. The after-tax amount will vary depending on the value of the tax credits the couple has available to them and where they live, due to different provincial rates across the country. An Ontario couple with only basic personal tax credits will have after-tax combined income of about $94,800, based on 2009 tax rates. If we use the three-month formula, they should have at least $23,700 in their emergency fund.

In contrast, a single person living in Nova Scotia who has a taxable income of only $35,000 a year and an after-tax income of $28,300 would need a minimum emergency reserve of about $7000.

These examples illustrate that there is no "right" amount for everyone. Much depends on your personal situation. Income is not the only factor to consider; you must also take into account your financial risk level. A single-income family whose breadwinner is an autoworker in Ontario should try to put more money aside than a couple in Alberta who both work in the public sector, because the risk of job loss is much higher in the automotive industry and the family does not have a second income to fall back on. A family whose main wage earner has a history of illness should have a larger emergency fund than one in which the primary earner is healthy. Families with children need to have more money in reserve than those who are childless.

Putting some cash aside each month for an emergency fund may seem daunting when you're planning a budget. But if you actually have to draw on the fund at some point, you will be thankful you made the effort. So where do you find the money?

I said earlier that commitment is half the battle when it comes to creating an emergency fund. The other half is execution. One way to achieve this goal is to set up a pre-authorized savings plan at your financial institution. Tell them to put aside 3 percent to 5 percent of your income each month (whatever you decide is appropriate) and deposit it into your TFSA. Even if the amount is small, I urge you to start the process. Then add to your savings every time a family member gets a salary increase or you receive some windfall money, such as a tax refund.

Since everyone is allowed to set up a TFSA, a couple could put as much as $10,000 into their plans each year. That is a good start toward an emergency fund; for a family with a low financial risk, it might even be enough.

Investment Options

Once you've started saving for an emergency fund, the question is where to invest the cash. There are two priorities to take into account. The first is safety: This is your "rainy day" money, so you don't want to put it at risk. The stock market meltdown that we experienced in the fall/winter of 2008–2009 was a painful reminder of the dangers of aggressive investing.

Your second priority is accessibility. Unless the money is available to you immediately, you don't have a true emergency fund.

This means you should not invest in any type of locked-in security, such as a non-redeemable guaranteed investment certificate. While such GICs are safe (they are covered by deposit insurance up to the legal limit) and offer more attractive interest rates than savings accounts, they will tie up your money for anywhere up to 10 years, depending on the maturity date (one-year to five-year terms are the most common). That makes them non-starters for emergency funds.

Redeemable GICs are a better choice in that you can get your money out before maturity if needed. However, you may pay an interest rate penalty if you make an early withdrawal, which may inhibit you from using the money even when it is badly needed.

Some financial institutions offer one-year cashable GICs that can be redeemed at any time without penalty. This makes them the most suitable type of GIC for an emergency fund, but there is one big drawback—the interest rate offered may be even less than that paid by a high-interest savings account.

A high-interest account is certainly a decent option for your emergency fund. Even during a period of low interest rates, the returns from these accounts will be higher than those offered by conventional savings accounts. You won't get rich with them but your money will be safe, you'll be able to withdraw it at any time, and the interest you earn will be tax-free. These accounts are especially good choices when interest rates are moving higher, since their rates are adjusted frequently.

If you decide this is the route you want to go, be sure to open your TFSA at a financial institution with a high-interest account that does not have a prohibitive minimum requirement. Check the rates being offered by various companies. For example, at the time of writing, Royal Bank was paying 0.75 percent on its RBC High Interest eSavings Account while ING DIRECT was offering 1.2 percent on its Investment Savings Account. Some people will forgo the extra interest for the convenience of dealing with their current bank. But look at it this way: The ING account was actually paying 60 percent more than the RBC account at that point. That's a big differential! So do some comparison shopping before you make a commitment (rates change frequently). And make sure your account is covered by deposit insurance.

Money Market Funds

If you want to aim for a slightly higher return, a money market fund (MMF) could be the answer. MMFs invest in short-term securities with an average term to maturity of less than 90 days (although they may hold notes with maturities out to one year). To qualify as a Canadian money market fund, at least 95 percent of the assets must be invested in Canadian-dollar securities.

MMFs have long been considered to be almost risk-free. However, nothing should be taken for granted these days. Even theoretically safe short-term notes can lose some or all of their value, and MMFs are not protected by deposit insurance. In 2007, National Bank had to put up $2 billion to bail out its MMFs as well as some Altamira funds after it was caught holding tainted asset-backed commercial paper (ABCP) in the wake of the U.S. sub-prime mortgage crash.

The Canadian Securities Administrators (CSA), which brings together all the provincial regulators, announced in September 2008 that it was looking into the extent to which Canadian MMFs might be exposed to high-risk U.S. debt securities, such as short-term notes issued by failed Lehman Brothers and Washington Mutual. The "fact-finding review," as it was called, was conducted in association with the Investment Industry Regulatory Organization of Canada (IIROC), which has oversight responsibility for brokerage houses.

The announcement came after the U.S. government had to step in and guarantee MMFs in that country for losses up to $50 billion after the giant Reserve Primary Fund "broke the buck"—that is, it reduced its net asset value to less than $1 because of losses due to its position in Lehman Brothers notes. (Canadian MMFs normally have a net asset value of $10.)

The Ontario Securities Commission subsequently reported that the MMF review had determined there were "no material issues" that would cause concern. But the OSC did not provide any details of the study. As of fall 2009, no Canadian MMF appeared to be in difficulty and none had dropped below par. However, many mutual fund companies were reducing MMF fees and cutting sales commissions and trailers because low interest rates threatened to reduce returns to zero or below.

So don't automatically assume your money market fund is safe. Ask your financial adviser (or the fund company itself if you don't have an adviser) what type of assets are held by the MMF you are considering. Some funds are heavily invested in notes issued by small companies that could be at risk if another financial crisis materializes. If you are not satisfied with the quality of the assets in the fund, switch to another MMF or to a high-interest savings account, which will be covered by deposit insurance.

The safest MMFs are those that invest only in federal or provincial treasury bills or government-guaranteed securities. Most of the major banks offer T-bill funds.

Safety is obviously a priority when it comes to choosing an MMF, but there are other considerations. Not all money market funds are created equal. They may look alike, in the sense that they all have a fixed price of $10 and they all invest in short-term securities. But that's where the similarities end. In fact, there are some very good money market funds, some very bad ones, and a whole lot of mediocre ones. Obviously, you want a good one, so here's what to look for.

No sales commission. Never pay a sales commission to buy or sell money market fund units. There are plenty of good no-load funds around. I once received an email from a distraught investor whose adviser had put his money into two MMFs on a deferred sales charge (DSC) basis. That meant that if he wanted to withdraw cash within the first six years of holding, he would be dinged with a redemption charge. He blamed himself for not paying closer attention, but I blamed his financial adviser, who had obviously acted in his own interest (he got a commission this way) and not in the interest of his client. Don't allow yourself to fall into that trap. MMFs should be commission-free, in and out.

Low fees. Returns on money market funds are historically quite low, so it's important to select a fund that will give you the most bang for your buck. This means avoiding funds with high management expense ratios (MERs). These ratios represent the cost to the fund of management fees and expenses and they come right off your return. For example, if an MMF generates a gross profit of 2 percent in a given year and has an MER of 0.5 percent, your return is 1.5 percent. But if the MER is 1.5 percent (and some are even higher), your return is only 0.5 percent. Don't have your pocket picked in this way!

Whatever way you decide to build your emergency fund within a TFSA, always remember the two most important principles: Make sure that your money is safe and that you can get at it quickly if needed.

Action Summary

1. Every family should have an emergency fund. A TFSA offers an ideal way to build one.
2. Choose an investment that offers both safety and quick access to your money if it is needed.
3. Avoid GICs or any other security that locks you in for a long time.
4. If you invest in a money market fund, select one that has low ongoing fees and no sales commissions.

6

TFSAs or RRSPs: Which to Choose?

The first question many people are going to ask about TFSAs is whether they should use a Tax-Free Savings Account or an RRSP for retirement saving.

There's no easy answer. TFSAs provide a valuable new option for retirement planning, but how they are best used will depend on each person's circumstances.

To begin with, it's important to understand that TFSAs and RRSPs are two different creatures from a tax and savings perspective. In the jargon of economists, TFSAs are so-called TEE plans—taxed, exempt, exempt. That means the money going into the plan has already been taxed, but earnings within a TFSA are tax-exempt, as are all withdrawals.

In contrast, RRSPs are so-called EET plans—exempt, exempt, taxed. Contributions are tax-free because they generate an offsetting deduction. Investment income earned within an RRSP is also tax-free. But all the money that comes out is taxed at your marginal rate, regardless of its source. That means you'll pay more tax on capital gains and dividends earned within an RRSP than you would if those same profits were generated in a non-registered account.

In the Budget Papers that explained the TFSA concept in detail, the Department of Finance included an example that suggested there is no after-tax advantage in using either TFSAs or RRSPs for retirement savings. Based on their assumptions, both produced the same net after-tax return and both were equally superior to saving in a non-registered account. See below for the illustration they used.[1]

This example assumes a contribution of $1000 to each of three different accounts—a TFSA, an RRSP, and an unregistered

Net Proceeds from Saving in a TFSA Relative to Other Savings Vehicles

	TFSA	RRSP	Unregistered savings
Pre-tax income	$1000	$1000	$1000
Tax (40% rate)	$400	–	$400
Net contribution[1]	$600	$1000	$600
Investment income (20 years at 5.5%)	$1151	$1918	$707[2]
Gross proceeds (net contribution + investment income)	$1751	$2918	$1307
Tax (40% rate)	–	$1167	–
Net proceeds	$1751	$1751	$1307
Net annual after-tax rate of return[3] (%)	5.5	5.5	4.0

[1]Forgone consumption (saving) is $600 in all cases. In the RRSP case, the person contributes $1000 but receives a $400 reduction in tax, thereby sacrificing net consumption of $600.

[2]For the unregistered savings case, the tax rate on investment income is 28%, representing a weighted average tax rate on an investment portfolio comprised of 30% dividends, 30% capital gains, and 40% interest.

[3]Measured in relation to forgone consumption of $600. Assumes annual nominal pre-tax rate of return is 5.5% invested for 20 years.

investment plan. But it is important to read the first footnote to the table to understand the rationale the Department of Finance used for the after-tax rate of return calculation. The figure is not based on the amount invested but rather on what Finance defines as "forgone consumption." This is the amount actually saved.

In all cases, the investor starts with a gross $1000. With the TFSA and the unregistered account, $400 is taken by taxes, leaving $600 in savings. That's straightforward enough, but the RRSP calculation is more complex: It appears at first glance that $1000 is the amount saved because that's what is paid into the plan and no tax is assessed because of the deduction generated. But the accepted way to make apples-to-apples comparisons in such situations is to examine it from the perspective of how much money a person could have spent if he or she had not made an investment. Using this approach, the "forgone consumption" is $600 in all cases. So the calculation of returns in all three scenarios is based on $600, although that number does not show up on the Net Contribution line in the RRSP column. For consistency, I'll stay with that approach in the analysis that follows.

Referring to the Finance table, you'll see that it shows the average annual compound rate of return for both a TFSA and an RRSP is 5.5 percent and the tax rate going in and coming out is 40 percent.

But if you change those basic assumptions, the end result can be quite different. Let's manipulate the numbers and consider the various outcomes. We'll begin by assuming that the contributor's marginal tax rate is lower in retirement than when she was working. We'll consider only a TFSA versus an RRSP because the results in an unregistered account don't change. Here is what happens, again using the "forgone consumption" of $600 as the base.

Net Proceeds from Saving in a TFSA Relative to an RRSP When the Final Tax Rate Is Lower

	TFSA	RRSP
Pre-tax income	$1000	$1000
Tax (40% rate)	$400	–
Net contribution	$600	$1000
Investment income (20 years at 5.5%)	$1151	$1918
Gross proceeds (net contribution + investment income)	$1751	$2918
Tax (30% rate)	–	$875
Net proceeds	$1751	$2043
Net annual after-tax rate of return (%)	5.5	6.3

In this case, as the table shows, the RRSP is clearly the better choice. It produces an average annual compound rate of return of 6.3 percent over 20 years compared with 5.5 percent for a TFSA. This means that higher-income people who expect their tax rate to be lower after retirement should top up their RRSPs first before investing in a TFSA.

Now let's see what happens when the tax rate after retirement is higher than when a person was working.

Because the tax rate is lower, the "forgone consumption" in this case is $700, so that becomes the basis for the rate of return calculation. As the following table shows, a TFSA is the better choice in this case, with an average annual compound rate of return of 5.5 percent, versus 4.7 percent for an RRSP.

So, to sum up:

If you expect your tax rate after retirement to be the same as it is now, TFSAs and RRSPs will produce the same net result.

Net Proceeds from Saving in a TFSA Relative to an RRSP When the Final Tax Rate Is Higher

	TFSA	RRSP
Pre-tax income	$1000	$1000
Tax (30% rate)	$300	–
Net contribution	$700	$1000
Investment income (20 years at 5.5%)	$1342	$1918
Gross proceeds (net contribution + investment income)	$2042	$2918
Tax (40% rate)	–	$1167
Net proceeds	$2042	$1751
Net annual after-tax rate of return (%)	5.5	4.7

If you expect your tax rate after retirement to be less than it is now, top up your RRSP before opening a TFSA.

If you expect your tax rate after retirement to be higher than it is now, saving in a TFSA will produce a better return than making an RRSP contribution.

When TFSAs Are Clearly Better

There are certain situations in which TFSAs are clearly a better choice than RRSPs for retirement-planning purposes. Here are three of them:

Pension plan members. Anyone who belongs to a pension plan loses RRSP contribution room because of the "pension adjustment" (PA). This is a complex calculation that takes into account the amount contributed to a pension plan by you and your employer, as well as the retirement benefit you will eventually receive. The more generous the plan, the higher the PA will be.

Anyone with a defined benefit pension plan (one that provides guaranteed retirement income based on a combination of salary and years of service) is likely to have a high PA. People in higher income brackets may find they have little or no RRSP room left after the PA has been deducted.

In this situation, TFSAs offer a valuable new alternative for supplementing pension income. By making the maximum possible contribution each year, you can build a tax-paid nest egg that will provide extra income that can be used for travel, a home in the Sunbelt, helping your kids buy a first home, a grandchild's post-secondary education, or anything else you may want to do after you stop work.

There's another reason to set up a TFSA to add to your retirement savings: It's a form of pension insurance. In the past, North Americans took their pension plans for granted. Not any more. In recent years, many pension plans have been forced to cut benefits because the funding was no longer there to support them.

Financially troubled US Airways had to cut pension benefits for its pilots by as much as 70 percent. Other major American airlines have sought to do the same, as did Air Canada while it was under creditor protection (it didn't succeed). Bethlehem Steel went into bankruptcy, leaving behind US$3.6 billion in unpaid obligations to its plan.

The Pension Benefits Guaranty Corporation (PBGC), which provides limited support to U.S. pensioners who have had their payments cut or suspended, reported in May 2009 that it was in the red to the tune of US$35.2 billion for the first half of the fiscal year. Acting director Vince Snowbarger told the Senate Special Committee on Aging that the deficit was the largest in the agency's 35-year history. He said it was caused "primarily by a drop in interest rates and by plan terminations." And there was a risk matters could get even worse; the PBGC estimated auto sector pensions were underfunded by about US$77 billion, of which US$42 billion would be guaranteed in the event of plan terminations.

The bottom line is that pension plans in the United States are failing at an alarming rate, putting increasing pressure on an already cash-strapped government agency.

Don't be deluded into thinking this is just an American problem. It can happen here, and even the biggest Canadian plans are not immune. But in Canada, we have no equivalent to the PBGC. That means there is no government agency to protect you if your own pension plan runs into financial trouble. (Ontario has a provincial program, but the benefits it covers are minimal.)

In September 2008, the Ontario Teachers' Pension Plan, which has more than $100 billion in assets, asked its members to give up part of their inflation-protection indexing to help deal with a $12.7 billion funding deficit.[2] If it can happen to teachers, who's safe?

The message is, Take nothing for granted. TFSAs provide an opportunity to backstop your pension plan with what amounts to your own pension insurance policy. Take advantage of it.

Modest-income Canadians. As we saw in Chapter 2, the primary rationale for the C.D. Howe Institute's strong advocacy of TFSAs was to provide an alternative retirement savings program that would better meet the needs of low-income people.

In all its reports on the subject, the institute was critical of the way in which low-income savers were penalized by government policies when the time came to draw on their RRSP or RRIF accounts. The most scathing denouncement was contained in Dr. Richard Shillington's 2003 paper, *New Poverty Traps: Means Testing and Modest-Income Seniors.*

"The primary beneficiary of this saving will be the federal and provincial governments because most of the income from it will be confiscated by income-tested programs and income taxes," Shillington wrote. "To the extent that these households have been misled, they have been defrauded."[3]

The report makes a clear distinction between the value of RRSP saving for higher-income Canadians, who will ultimately benefit from their plans, and lower-income people, who will not. Shillington's message was that all those with less than $100,000 in retirement assets are "futile savers" because they will probably need financial support from governments after they stop work. Those benefits will be reduced or even eliminated if there is any income from RRSPs and RRIFs. (Remember: Every dollar in income from one of those plans reduces a Guaranteed Income Supplement benefit by 50 cents.)

Using a TFSA instead of an RRSP eliminates that problem, at least on the federal level. The federal government has ensured that TFSA withdrawals are not treated as income, nor will they be taken into account when calculating eligibility for GIS, tax credits, Employment Insurance, and so forth. (At the time of writing, most provinces still had to take action to provide similar treatment for programs they deliver.)

Clearly, anyone with a modest income should favour TFSAs over RRSPs for retirement-savings purposes, even when the amounts being put aside are small.

No earned income. You cannot make an RRSP contribution unless you have what the government calls "earned income." Mostly, this is money earned from employment, but some other types of income, such as rents and alimony, also qualify. Investment income does not qualify as earned income, nor do pension payments, whether from the government or from a private plan.

If you don't have any earned income, or if the amount is small, TFSAs become your retirement savings vehicle by default. That's because you don't need any earned income to make a TFSA contribution.

Years ago, the typical Canadian family had one wage earner, usually the husband. The wife remained at home and raised the couple's children. Such families are less common today, but they still exist. In this situation, the wife is not able to save independently for her retirement through an RRSP because she has no earned income. If the wife has no earned income, the husband can make a spousal contribution on her behalf, but spousal RRSPs have significant restrictions on the ability to withdraw funds.

Now she has an option: a TFSA. She does not need to have earned income to set up a personal retirement account. If she has some money of her own (perhaps from an inheritance from her parents), she can contribute some of it to the plan. Alternatively, her husband can give her the money to contribute, since income attribution rules will not apply in this case.

When RRSPs Are Better

There are some situations in which an RRSP is a better option than a TFSA—in fact, it may be the only choice. One example is a child or teenager with earned income. You must be 18 or older to open a TFSA, but there is no age limit for RRSPs. As long as a person has earned income, that person can have an RRSP account.

Most people don't realize this, so they pass up opportunities to encourage their children to put some of their earnings, however modest they may be, into an RRSP. For example, my granddaughter had a job at Canada's Wonderland, an amusement park north of Toronto, during the summer when she was 16. Her wages were modest, but they qualified as earned income for RRSP purposes. She was too young to open a TFSA, but she could contribute 18 percent of her earned income (the maximum allowed) to an RRSP. And she can defer claiming the tax deduction until she is working full-time and the deduction will be more worthwhile. Meanwhile, the money will be compounding inside her RRSP.

She earned about $2800 over the summer. That allowed her to contribute $500 to an RRSP. At the time, she had 49 years before she would reach age 65. At an average annual growth rate of 5 percent, that $500 would grow more than 10 times, to $5460.67 at the end of that time. It's just one more example of the magic of compounding.

First-Time Homebuyers

One of the most popular features of RRSPs is the Home Buyers' Plan (HBP). This program allows first-time homebuyers to borrow up to $25,000 from an RRSP interest-free and to pay the money back over 15 years. Hundreds of thousands of Canadians have made use of it since the plan was introduced in 1992, originally as a temporary measure to help a beleaguered housing market. Now aspiring homeowners face the dilemma of whether to use an RRSP or a TFSA as the savings vehicle for their down payment.

An RRSP allows you to reach your financial goal more quickly because you do not pay tax on RRSP contributions (you get an offsetting tax deduction) and your money therefore accumulates faster. Take a look at the following chart. It shows how much money would be accumulated in each plan based on $3500 a year in before-tax income. I've assumed an annual rate of return of 5 percent and for purposes of the TFSA contributions a marginal tax rate of 30 percent on the $3500.

Home Ownership Savings: RRSPs versus TFSAs

Year	RRSP	TFSA
1	$3675	$2573
2	$7534	$5274
3	$11,585	$8110
4	$15,840	$11,088
5	$20,307	$14,215
6	$24,997	$17,498

At the end of six years, you will have accumulated almost $25,000 in the RRSP and can take maximum advantage of the HBP. The value of the TFSA, however, is only $17,498 because you were only able to contribute $2450 a year after tax. It will be an additional two years before the TFSA reaches the $25,000 level, by which time you'll have your house.

If you had to withdraw the money outright from the RRSP to buy the home, it would be a different story because the $25,000 would be taxed coming out. But with the HBP (as well as the Lifelong Learning Plan, which allows interest-free RRSP loans for continuing education), no tax is assessed on withdrawals as long as the loan is repaid on schedule or faster.

So, if saving for a first home is your number-one priority, the RRSP is the best way to do it. If you want to move even faster, use your RRSP refund to open a TFSA and save both ways.

Large Contributions

Because of the low contribution limits on TFSAs, big savers are better off using RRSPs because they can shelter more money from taxes. The maximum RRSP contribution for the 2010 tax year is $22,000, more than four times the amount you can put into a TFSA.

Of course, you're allowed to do both—the two types of plans can be used in tandem to build a supersized retirement nest egg.

Action Summary

1. Contribute to an RRSP before a TFSA if you expect to be taxed at a lower rate after retirement. If your tax rate is likely to be higher than it is now, use the TFSA first.
2. If you are a member of a pension plan, contribute to TFSAs to supplement your retirement savings, especially if you have little or no RRSP room.
3. If you are planning to buy a house, save for your down payment in an RRSP rather than a TFSA and make use of the RRSP Home Buyers' Plan.

7

Tax Relief for Seniors

Although statistics tell us that many retired Canadians live below the poverty line, a lot of retirees are doing very well for themselves.

According to data published by the Canada Revenue Agency, about 4.4 million Canadians over age 65 filed tax returns for 2007 (the latest year for which figures were available at the time of writing). Of these, almost 2.5 million (57 percent) reported taxable income, in the amount of $156.8 billion. That works out to an average of almost $63,000 per taxable filer.[1] Clearly, these folks are doing all right.

The other side of the coin is that almost half of older people (43 percent) live on incomes that are so low they don't even meet the minimum threshold for paying tax. In reality, the percentage is probably much higher because the data only covers tax filers. How many more seniors don't bother to submit a return because their incomes are low or non-existent?

Compare that with the average income of tax-paying retirees and it's immediately apparent that there is a huge gap between the two groups. TFSAs won't bridge that chasm, although over time they may reduce the income disparity by giving lower-income people more incentive to save. But the first ones to benefit are those on the higher-income side of the retirement divide.

I frequently receive emails from older readers who are angry because the payments from their Registered Retirement Income Funds (RRIFs) are taxed at such a high rate (RRIFs are the programs used to generate income from RRSP savings). Some are so outraged, they say that if they had realized how much tax they'd have to pay they never would have bothered saving for retirement in the first place.

My response to such complaints is always the same: You're lucky. Anyone who has to pay high taxes does so because he or she enjoys above-average income. There are worse things to worry about in retirement than making too much money. I doubt many of the complainers would want to trade places with someone at the other end of the income scale.

That said, I understand the desire of these folks to cut their tax bills. And as long as it can be done legally, I encourage them to go ahead. TFSAs offer several ways to achieve that goal. The savings aren't necessarily dramatic, but every little bit helps.

Advance Planning

As we saw in the last chapter, anyone who expects their tax rate to be higher in retirement should be saving in a TFSA rather than an RRSP. There are a number of situations in which that might happen. Here are three examples:

You start a business. A growing number of people move on to a new career after they stop working. This may be anything from consulting to dog breeding. When combined with pension and investment income, the additional cash flow could push these people into a higher tax bracket.

Consider the example of a B.C. government worker with the provincial Ministry of Small Business and Revenue. Her pre-retirement income was $70,000, and her marginal tax rate was about 30 percent. She retires at 65 with a pension equal to 75 percent of her salary, or $52,500. She draws CPP benefits of $10,600 a year and Old Age Security of $6200, bringing the total to $69,300—almost as much as when she stopped working. She then decides to start a tax-preparation service for small companies. It turns out to be highly successful and generates an additional $25,000 in net income. Her marginal tax rate has just jumped to more than 38 percent!

If this woman has saved any money in an RRSP, she will have to pay more tax when it comes out than the value of the refund she received when she made the contribution. Had she put the same amount into a TFSA, she would end up ahead.

You receive a windfall. Everyone dreams of winning a lottery, but the most likely windfall you'll receive is an inheritance. As baby boomers approach retirement, many will lose their last surviving parent and the estate will pass to the next generation. Even after the government takes its tax cut, billions of dollars worth of savings, real estate, and insurance will end up in the hands of adult children who are themselves close to leaving the workforce.

In some cases, the inheritance may be worth hundreds of thousands of dollars or even more. When invested, this money will generate returns that, when added to other income, will move the heirs into higher tax brackets. To illustrate, a $500,000 inheritance that earns 6 percent a year will add $30,000 to a person's income. That's enough to push an Ontario resident who had been receiving $60,000 a year in taxable income from a marginal tax rate of 31.15 percent all the way to 43.41 percent (2009 rates). While there won't be enough TFSA room available for several years to shelter a large inheritance, anyone who anticipates receiving a bequest should open a plan now and be ready to move as much money as possible into it when the time comes.

You plan to move to a higher-tax province. Consider the case of a Nova Scotian who went to Alberta to work in the oil sands industry. He has made good money, slightly more than $100,000 a year. But because Alberta tax rates are so low, his marginal tax rate is only 36 percent. Now he's retiring and wants to return to Halifax where his family still lives. He'll receive less income in retirement— his pension, CPP, OAS, and a small amount of investment income will add up to about $87,000 a year in taxable income. But because tax rates are much higher in Nova Scotia, his marginal rate will actually rise to 44.34 percent.

In all these situations, starting a TFSA during the working years will produce better post-retirement after-tax results than an RRSP.

After You've Retired

After you've fully retired, the TFSA/RRSP dilemma may still come into play. We are allowed to have RRSPs and to make contributions to them until the end of the year in which we turn 71. Even retirees with no earned income can take advantage of this situation if they have unused carry-forward room, which many do. Check your most recent Notice of Assessment from the Canada Revenue Agency to find out whether you do too. But even if you have RRSP contribution room, is it worthwhile using it now that TFSAs are available?

Perhaps, but you need to look at the situation carefully. For starters, how much money is involved? You can contribute only $5000 a year to a TFSA. If you have more unused RRSP contribution room than your TFSA limit and you have the necessary cash, you should make use of the RRSP. Remember, the more money you can tax-shelter and the sooner you can do it, the better.

Next, consider whether you expect your tax rate to be lower, higher, or about the same after age 71. If it is likely to be higher, forget about the RRSP unless you would rather exchange a small tax deduction now for a higher tax bill later. If you anticipate no change, it's a toss-up, but since you can only keep the RRSP for a few years longer anyway, you may want to go right to a TFSA.

You should also look at your exposure to the Old Age Security clawback, which cuts in when net income exceeds $66,335 (2009 rates). This onerous surtax grabs back 15 cents of every dollar of net income that exceeds the threshold. And that's on top of your regular tax rate. The effect is that a Quebec resident who receives OAS payments and has taxable income of $70,000 is being socked at a marginal rate of more than 53 percent! Since RRSP and RRIF payments count as income but TFSA withdrawals do not, anyone who expects to be subject to the clawback should opt for a TFSA.

For modest-income retirees (anyone earning less than $30,000 a year), it's a no-brainer. Choose the TFSA over an RRSP. This ensures you won't compromise your eligibility for the Guaranteed Income Supplement or various federal tax credits.

Most people over the age of 71 won't have to choose between a TFSA and an RRSP, but there are exceptions. Suppose a 72-year-old married woman (who can no longer hold an RRSP) has earned income and/or unused carry-forward room. Her disabled husband is 69 and is therefore still RRSP-eligible. In this case, the woman has a choice: She can make a contribution to a spousal RRSP or put money into a TFSA.

The key consideration here is what her husband's tax rate is likely to be in the future compared to her current marginal rate. In this case, the odds are that the husband's rate will be very low—in fact, he may not have to pay any tax at all once he claims the personal and disability credits. So the spousal RRSP would be the right choice—she gets a deduction now, and the money comes out of the husband's plan later as income in his hands. That means it will be taxed at a low rate or perhaps not at all.

RRIF/LIF Withdrawals

Once an RRSP is converted to a RRIF or a life income fund (LIF: a locked-in account funded by pension plan money), the federal government requires that a minimum amount be taken out of the plan annually. This is based on a percentage of the market value of the plan on January 1 of each year. The minimum percentage you are required to withdraw increases with age; at 70, it is 5 percent, but by the time you reach 75, it is up to 7.85 percent.

Canadians who have other sources of income, such as an employer pension, frequently complain that these forced withdrawals put them in a position of taking out more money than they need, thereby pushing them into a higher tax bracket. The tax implications are especially onerous in cases where RRIF/LIF withdrawals add enough to a person's income to move them over the OAS clawback threshold. The new pension-splitting rules may ease the tax situation for some couples, but most retirees would prefer to have greater flexibility in deciding how much to take out of a RRIF or LIF each year.

Two decades from now, TFSAs should have eased the problem because they allow future generations the flexibility to diversify their retirement savings, thereby reducing the dependence on taxable RRIFs. But what about today?

Unfortunately, TFSAs do nothing to ease the immediate tax bite of RRIF/LIF withdrawals. What they can do is to shelter future investment income from the tax folks.

Prior to TFSAs, there was no inexpensive tax-shelter program for Canadians over age 71. Universal life policies offer tax protection, but they are expensive, and if you don't already have one, your health may disqualify you. TFSAs change the landscape.

Retirees can now move $5000 a year (so $10,000 per couple) of unneeded RRIF/LIF withdrawals into TFSA accounts. Yes, they'll still pay tax on the money as it comes out of the RRIF/LIF, but at least they will be able to ensure they will not have to pay any more tax on the future investment income they earn.

Since older people have a shorter life expectancy, the benefits of TFSAs aren't as great as for people in their twenties. However, Statistics Canada tells us that a Canadian male aged between 70 and 74 can expect to live another 13.7 years, while a woman in the same age group can expect to survive another 16.7 years.[2]

So let's assume that a woman who is now age 70 starts contributing $5000 a year from unneeded RRIF withdrawals to a TFSA. She continues to do this for the next five years, during which time the investment income accrues at an average annual compound rate of 6 percent. By age 75, she has a tax-free nest egg worth $29,877. At this point, she finds that she needs the full amount of her RRIF withdrawal to live on, so she stops contributing her RRIF withdrawals to the TFSA and simply allows the money in the TFSA to continue compounding. By the time she is 80, the TFSA will be worth $39,982. At age 85, the woman will find that her TFSA has grown to $53,504. At this point, her RRIF may be almost depleted, but she now has the TFSA to fall back on and she won't need to withdraw as much to live on because no tax will be withheld. If she doesn't need the money in the TFSA, it will make a nice inheritance for her children or grandchildren.

So even if you are in your seventies, don't ignore the tax-saving potential of these new plans. Sure, it would have been nice if they'd been available when you entered the workforce so many years ago, but better late than never.

Action Summary

1. If you are not yet retired, give careful thought to what your income is likely to be after you stop work and how much tax you will pay. It will help you decide whether to make any more RRSP contributions.
2. If you plan to move after you retire, check the tax rates in the province to which you are relocating.
3. Invest any unneeded RRIF withdrawal money in a TFSA, up to the annual limit.

8

Education Savings

Which type of savings plan should you choose for a child's or grandchild's university education? At first glance, there are a lot of similarities between Tax-Free Savings Accounts (TFSAs) and Registered Education Savings Plans (RESPs).

Both are funded with tax-paid money—you don't receive a deduction for your contributions.

Both tax-shelter investment income earned within the plan.

Both allow the tax-free withdrawal of contributions at any time.

Both have a contribution year-end of December 31, unlike RRSPs which allow you 60 days after the end of a calendar year to get your money into the plan.

But that's where the resemblance ends. RESPs come with several strings and conditions, as well as with government-sponsored savings incentives. TFSAs are much more flexible, but Ottawa doesn't kick in any extra cash to encourage you to use them.

So the answer of whether to choose a TFSA or an RESP for education savings is not as clear-cut as you might expect.

Registered Education Savings Plans (RESPs)

Let's begin by looking at the pros and cons of RESPs. These plans have been around for years but were seldom used until the federal government decided to give them a boost by creating the Canada Education Savings Grant (CESG). This is a program operated by Human Resources and Social Development Canada that adds a 20 percent bonus to your annual RESP contribution to a maximum of $500 a year (or $1000 if you have unused grant room from past years). The lifetime limit is $7200 per child and there are no income restrictions on these grants. They are paid directly into the RESP.

In addition, modest-income families get an extra grant on the first $500 they contribute to an RESP each year. This can be either 10 percent or 20 percent on $500—in other words, $50 or $100 on top of the basic grant. The lower the income, the greater the amount, although families with net income as high as about $78,000 can qualify for this extra grant. The qualifying net income of the child's family for a year will generally be the same as the income used to determine eligibility for the Canada Child Tax Benefit.

These grants are paid until the year the child (technically known as the "plan beneficiary") turns 17. But there are some conditions. Grants will be paid only on behalf of beneficiaries who are 16 or 17 if the RESP was set up before they turned 16 and a minimum of $100 a year was contributed to the plan for four years. The other option is to put at least $2000 into the plan before the beneficiary turns age 16 (which could all be contributed in a single year or spread out).

What this boils down to is that for older children to qualify for the CESG, the RESP must be set up before the end of the calendar year in which the child turns 15 and the required contributions must be made.

The CESG is a powerful incentive to use RESPs and can add thousands of dollars to the end value of a plan. For example, suppose a parent opens an RESP for a newborn and contributes enough money each year to earn the basic grant. In the child's 15th year, the maximum lifetime grant of $7200 will be reached. If the money in the RESP earns 6 percent annually, by the time the child is 18, the added value of the CESG plus accumulated earnings will be more than $14,000.

There's more! Families who are entitled to the National Child Benefit (NCB) may qualify for up to $2000 in additional government incentives through what is known as the Canada Learning Bond (CLB). This provides an additional $500 for children born in 2004 or later, plus $25 in the first year to help pay for the cost of setting up an RESP. After that, an additional $100 a year will be deposited into the RESP for up to 15 years as long as the family qualifies for the NCB.

No wonder RESPs have become more popular in recent years!

Another advantage offered by these plans is contribution flexibility. In the past, parents or grandparents were restricted to a maximum annual contribution of $4000. Now there is no annual maximum—the only limitation is that the lifetime amount contributed on behalf of any one child cannot exceed $50,000. (Remember, however, that only the first $2500 contributed qualifies for the CESG in that year.) You are allowed to make contributions until the plan beneficiary turns 31.

Now let's consider the drawbacks of RESPs.

Income taxed on withdrawal. Although contributions to an RESP can be withdrawn tax-free at any time, investment income earned within a plan is taxed when it comes out. These are called educational assistance payments (EAPs). Fortunately, such withdrawals are deemed to be income received by the student, not the contributor. Since a university student is unlikely to have much income from other sources, tax payable on RESP withdrawals may not be significant—indeed, the student may have no taxable income at all once the tuition and education tax credits are applied.

Money must be used for education. The rules governing RESP withdrawals are fairly loose. As long as the end use relates to post-secondary education, almost anything goes. Withdrawals can be used to pay for tuition, residence, books, travel, athletics, even a computer. And there is nothing in the rules that says the beneficiary must go to a Canadian university; an RESP can be used to finance a Harvard education if the student can gain admission. But if the beneficiary does not go on to post-secondary studies, there's a problem. This is where the real downside of RESPs comes into play.

Penalties if a child quits school. The major risk of RESPs is the extremely high tax penalty that contributors face if the plan beneficiary decides not to pursue a post-secondary education. These plans are specifically intended for education saving, and the government hits contributors with hefty taxes if things don't work out that way (most RESPs must be wound up by their 35th-anniversary date).

You might argue that this is inherently unfair. After all, it is not the fault of the parents if their daughter decides that university isn't her thing or if her marks aren't good enough to gain admission. They did everything they were supposed to, dutifully cutting back their spending so they could put money aside for her schooling. Why should they be penalized when she decides she would rather take a job at the local mall or travel around the world? After all, the government doesn't punish RRSP investors if they don't use the money to fund their retirement.

If a child decides not to go on to post-secondary education, the cost to the plan and the contributor can amount to thousands of dollars. The contributor may withdraw the contributions tax-free but will have to repay all the money received from the Canada Education Savings Grant and the Canada Learning Bond to the government.

The money that remains in the RESP will consist of the investment income earned over the years. In a case where $2500 a year was contributed to a plan over 18 years that earned 6 percent annually, the investment earnings will amount to almost $37,000.

Once the contributor takes this money out of an RESP that is not used by the beneficiary, it is called an accumulated income payment (AIP). If the contributing parent or grandparent has an RRSP and enough contribution room available, he or she can move the AIP there directly without having to pay tax on it (or use a spousal plan). But if an RRSP transfer is not feasible, the tax hit is fierce.

In that case, the AIP will be added to your regular income for the year in which it is received. That means it will be taxed at your marginal rate. But the government wants more. You'll be hit with an extra 20 percent penalty on top of that (12 percent in Quebec), which pushes the effective tax rate to almost confiscatory levels.

To put this in perspective, let's look at the case of an Ontario father who has a taxable income of $60,000 a year. The family scrimped and saved in an RESP to send their son (an only child) to university, but he was academically challenged and dropped out of high school in his senior year. The parents were not only disappointed with his decision but were left with the problem of winding up the RESP. After repaying the government grants and withdrawing their principal, the parents found the RESP had $25,000 remaining in it. Since neither parent had any RRSP contribution room available, the money had to be withdrawn as an AIP.

Using 2009 rates, the normal tax payable on the $25,000 withdrawal would be $9277, based on the father's regular income. But the 20 percent penalty would add $5000 to the bill, bringing the total to $14,277. That works out to an effective tax rate of 57.1 percent on the AIP. There is no reasonable justification for this, but it is how the system operates. The result is that RESPs are something of a gamble, despite all the government support.

Scholarship trusts. There is one other risk to RESPs that relates directly to the type of plan used. Scholarship trusts have aggressively marketed RESP programs for years, and some have been quite successful. Students who meet the qualifications and use the plans to go through university can receive generous grants.

But the trusts charge hefty upfront fees, and families that decide to drop out of the plan early can end up losing thousands of dollars. So they carry a double risk—first, that the child may not go on to college and second, that the parents may not be able to keep up with the payment schedule.

Tax-Free Savings Accounts and Education Savings

There are no bells and whistles if you decide to use a TFSA rather than an RESP to save for a child's education. You get no government support—the only money in the plan is what you contribute.

But there is also no risk. The money that accumulates in a TFSA can be used for any purpose at all. The government won't sock it to you if your child or grandchild decides not to go to university.

This flexibility means that there is no pressure on a child to do something he or she doesn't want to do. It also means that the money you've accumulated can be used for some other purpose, such as providing a down payment on a first home or paying for a wedding.

What makes the decision so difficult is that there is no way of knowing when a child is young whether he or she will eventually go on to post-secondary education. Surprisingly, there appears to be no data that tells us what percentage of children in Canada who start elementary school eventually proceed to some form of post-secondary education. When I put that question to the Ontario Ministry of Education, I was informed by a researcher that "the requested data will be available starting 2017–2018 as the ministry started collecting elementary student level data in 2005–2006 school year for the first time." That's not much help to a parent who is trying to decide right now whether to risk opening an RESP.

A report published in 2006 by Colleges Ontario found that 52 percent of Ontario high school graduates enrolled in college or university.[1] However, this refers only to students who actually finished high school.

If the federal government were to eliminate the 20-percent tax penalty, parents would not be faced with such a difficult choice. But unless that happens, Canadians will be forced to make a decision when a child is very young that they may come to regret years later.

From a strictly financial perspective, an RESP is the better choice if the plan beneficiary is young. The following table compares the value of an RESP and a TFSA at the end of various time frames. It assumes an annual contribution of $2500 plus the payment of the basic CESG to the RESP at a rate of $500 a year to a maximum of $7200. The average annual compound rate of return is 6 percent.

RESPs versus TFSAs (1)

Years	TFSA	RESP	RESP gain
5	$14,938	$17,926	+$2988
10	$34,929	$41,915	+$6986
15	$61,681	$73,700	+$12,019
20	$97,482	$113,565	+$16,083

Assumption: Average annual compound rate of return is 6%.

As you can see, the RESP offers a significant financial advantage, and the longer the plan is in existence, the greater the differential. However, the only reason the RESP generates more money is the contribution from the Canada Education Savings Grant. Without the CESG, the end result for both plans would be the same.

But remember, if a child does not have an RESP opened for her before the end of the year she turns 15, she will not be eligible for the CESG. This changes the equation for people who come late to education savings. With the CESG removed from the calculation, the advantage shifts to using a TFSA rather than an RESP for the following reasons:

Same financial result. Both plans will accumulate the same amount of money, assuming equal contributions and rates of return.

No withdrawal restrictions. TFSA savings don't have to be used for education purposes. If the child decides not to go the post-secondary route, the money can be spent on something else or simply left in the plan to accumulate.

No tax on withdrawals. Although the tax rate on most RESP withdrawals will be low or non-existent, TFSA withdrawals are completely tax-free.

However, keep in mind that only $5000 a year can be contributed to a TFSA, whereas there is no annual limit on RESPs. If the goal is to quickly build a large education fund for an older child who is certain to go on to post-secondary education, consider using the two plans in combination.

A TFSA may also be a better choice for people with a lot of money. If the parent or grandparent wants to contribute more than $50,000 to an education savings plan (the maximum allowed per child in an RESP) and the contributions are spread over several years, a TFSA produces a better return in the end.

Let's look at a scenario of a child born in 2010. The parents want to save $5000 a year for her education. Which plan works better? After 10 years, the lifetime RESP maximum is reached and the contributions stop. But since there is no such restriction on TFSAs, the payments continue.

The RESP receives the maximum $500 grant each year for 10 years for a total of $5000. (Since there is no accumulated grant room, the parents lose out on the remaining $2200 of CESG payments.) The result is in the following table.

Thanks to the CESG payment, the RESP jumps into an early lead. But after year 10, when contributions cease, the TFSA starts to close the gap. At the end of year 12, the values of both plans are

RESPs versus TFSAs (2)

Years	TFSA	RESP	RESP gain/loss
5	$29,877	$32,864	+$2987
10	$69,858	$76,844	+$6986
15	$123,363	$102,835	−$20,528
20	$194,964	$137,616	−$57,348

Assumption: Average annual compound rate of return is 6%.

almost equal. After that, the TFSA moves ahead and the gap continues to widen in each subsequent year.

However, keep in mind that twice as much money is contributed by the parents or grandparents to the TFSA as to the RESP. The RESP is actually more efficient because of the CESG, even though the amount of money in the plan after 20 years is $57,000 less.

The bottom line is that if the child is eligible for the Canada Education Savings Grant, an RESP is a more efficient way to save for university from a financial perspective. But each family will have to decide whether it is willing to live with the tax risk involved if the student does not choose to pursue post-secondary education.

Action Summary

1. For young children, open an RESP instead of a TFSA for education savings because of the added benefit of the CESG. However, be aware of the potential tax risk if the child does not go on to post-secondary education.
2. For older children who do not already have RESPs, use a TFSA to save for their education unless you anticipate making contributions of more than $5000 a year.

9

Save Taxes by Splitting Income

The Government of Canada has never liked the concept of income splitting, perhaps because it would cost the federal Treasury too much in lost revenue. This means that Canadian couples end up paying a lot more in taxes than, for example, American couples, who are allowed to file joint returns.

The extra tax we pay can add up to thousands of dollars a year per couple. Take a look at the following table. It shows how much money could be saved in taxes each year by Ontario couples of various income levels if full income splitting were allowed in Canada, assuming both were earning the same amount. The figures are based on 2009 tax rates. I used the online Personal Tax Calculator provided by the accounting firm of Ernst & Young to crunch the numbers.[1]

The table clearly illustrates that if couples were allowed to file joint tax returns, the savings would be significant. Moreover, the last column shows that such a change in policy would provide the greatest relief to lower-income families, leaving them with more after-tax income. In some cases, this might be enough to remove them from social welfare rolls.

The Effect of Income Splitting

Family taxable income	Tax (current system)	Tax (income splitting)	Savings	Tax reduction
$30,000	$4350	$2344	$2006	46.1%
$40,000	$6726	$4490	$2236	33.2%
$50,000	$9841	$6594	$3247	33.0%
$60,000	$12,956	$8700	$4256	32.8%
$80,000	$20,062	$13,452	$6610	32.9%
$100,000	$28,744	$19,682	$9062	31.5%
$150,000	$51,254	$35,846	$15,408	30.1%

The Conservative Party has dabbled with income splitting, which suggests that we may be slowly moving in that direction. In 2007, new rules took effect that allowed pension income to be divided between spouses or partners. However, the regulations make the program so complicated that even tax professionals had trouble figuring out the optimum split in individual situations in its first year.

The Conservatives' 2008 election platform contained a promise to extend income splitting to caregivers of family members with disabilities. But that has yet to be implemented and would apply to only a small number of people. For the great majority of Canadians, income splitting remains an elusive dream.

In addition to limiting income splitting to just a few situations, the Canada Revenue Agency has strict rules that prevent the transfer of assets from one spouse to another (or to minor children) for purposes of dividing investment income. Under these "income attribution" regulations, any dividends, capital gains, or interest earned in this way must be declared for tax purposes by the person who provided the money originally.

For example, suppose a husband wanted to give $50,000 to his wife as a gift. The transfer of money in itself is not illegal and does not attract tax. But now let's assume the wife invests the cash and earns 5 percent on it, which works out to $2500 in the first year. That income must be declared on the husband's tax return, not hers.

TFSAs are a game changer. It will take time, but over several years, a couple will be able to put together a meaningful income-splitting plan, at least as far as their investments are concerned.

The key that makes this possible is that the Canada Revenue Agency waives the attribution rules when the money is used to invest in a TFSA. Annex 4 of the 2008 Budget Plan states,

> If an individual transfers property to the individual's spouse or common-law partner, the income tax rules generally treat any income earned on that property as income of the individual. An exception to these "attribution rules" will allow individuals to take advantage of the TFSA contribution room available to them using funds provided by their spouse or common-law partner: the rules will not apply to income earned in a TFSA that is derived from such contributions.[2]

This means that even if a wife has no income and no assets, the husband can transfer up to $5000 a year to her (based on the initial contribution limit) to invest in a TFSA. As her plan builds, the effect will be to effectively switch investment income from his hands to hers for tax purposes.

Over a period of 10 years, this strategy would shift $50,000 in capital from the husband to the wife. Assuming an average annual return of 6 percent, the value of the wife's TFSA at the end of that time will be $67,852. Let's also assume the husband's income is $85,000 a year. Using TFSAs works out to a tax saving for the husband of $5429.[3] The figure is based on an investment in a diversified portfolio in which the investment earnings are 40 percent interest, 30 percent dividends, and 30 percent capital gains.

People with more modest incomes won't save quite as much because they will be in a lower tax bracket. But even if the husband earns only $45,000 a year, the cumulative tax saving would be almost $4300.

The greatest beneficiaries will be young people because the longer the time frame, the more investment income is earned in the plan and the greater the tax savings.

Let's consider the case of a couple who are both 30 years old and who adopt twin girls. They decide that the husband will be a stay-at-home dad while the wife remains on in her well-paying job as a human resources manager for a medium-sized oil company where she earns $105,000 annually.

In order to move some income into his hands, she gives her husband $5000 a year to invest in a TFSA. He is quite knowledge-able about investing and succeeds in generating an average annual return of 8 percent over the years. Assuming her income stays constant and tax rates don't change (which of course they will, but this is an illustration), the amount of tax saved over 30 years will be a whopping $193,240. And that's just the tax they've kept in their own hands! The total value of his TFSA at the end of that time will be $588,637.

The tax savings would be exactly the same if the wife had simply opened her own TFSA instead. However, this strategy gives the couple double the tax-saving power. If she makes the same contributions to her own TFSA and achieves similar returns, their combined tax savings after 30 years is $386,480!

Of course, this couple's financial position would be even better if full income splitting were allowed. But for now, this is a pretty good start.

Action Summary

1. Use TFSAs to split investment income between you and your spouse, potentially saving you thousands of tax dollars over the years.
2. Get your spouse to open a plan as well, to double the tax-saving potential.

10

Passing On

I receive dozens of emails each year from older people asking about how they can leave more money to their children and grandchildren when they pass on.

There are ways to achieve this, but they typically involve complex legal structures, such as trusts, and they can be costly. Unless there is a great deal of money involved, it may not be worth the time and expense.

In some ways, Canadians are better off than our neighbours to the south when it comes to passing on assets to the next generation. The United States imposes hefty succession taxes on its well-to-do citizens. Right now, these are being reduced, but the tax rates will revert to previous levels in 2011 unless Congress moves to abolish them permanently. Given the current state of the U.S. Treasury, that does not seem likely.

We have no estate tax as such in Canada. However, our governments have figured out other ways to grab a large chunk of your money when you die that can be almost as onerous.

This happens when the wealth transfer is to the next generation. Your assets can pass to your spouse or common-law partner after your death with no tax implications. The big hit occurs when the last surviving spouse or partner dies and the estate is transferred to the children or other heirs. For most families, the tax bite at this stage occurs in two ways.

Crystallizing of capital gains at death. When you die, all your investments are deemed to have been sold at fair market value. This means that any profits you have on stocks, mutual funds, real property (other than the principal residence), bonds, and so forth are treated as taxable capital gains on your final tax return. (Yes, the government requires that you, or more precisely, your estate, file a tax return even after you are dead.)

Closing of all registered plans. Any registered retirement plans (RRSPs, RRIFs, LIFs) that you own are considered to have been terminated on the day you die. All the money in the accounts is treated as personal income on your final tax return.

This can result in a huge tax bill because all the extra income in registered retirement accounts will attract the top marginal rate, which in some provinces is more than 48 percent. TFSAs are not subject to this tax risk.

The following table shows how much tax could be assessed on a final return depending on where in Canada the deceased lived and on the taxable value of the registered retirement accounts in the estate. Keep in mind that there is no tax on the assets of an RRSP, RRIF, and so on that pass to a surviving spouse.

The figures are based on 2009 rates and do not make provision for special tax treatment, such as the 50 percent capital gains inclusion rate. They are provided by the Ernst & Young online Personal Tax Calculator.[1] They do not include provincial probate fees.

Potential Taxes on Registered Retirement Accounts

Value of Plan Assets

Domicile	$100,000	$250,000	$500,000	$750,000	$1,000,000
British Columbia	$25,757	$90,519	$199,769	$309,019	$418,269
Alberta	$26,665	$84,378	$181,878	$279,378	$376,878
Saskatchewan	$29,081	$94,000	$204,000	$314,000	$424,000
Manitoba	$31,144	$99,956	$215,956	$331,956	$447,956
Ontario	$28,036	$96,863	$212,888	$328,913	$444,938
Quebec	$32,619	$104,290	$224,840	$345,390	$465,940
New Brunswick	$30,710	$98,760	$213,760	$328,760	$443,760
Nova Scotia	$32,117	$103,703	$224,328	$344,953	$465,578
Prince Edward Island	$31,184	$101,451	$219,876	$338,301	$456,726
Newfoundland and Labrador	$29,781	$95,743	$206,993	$318,243	$429,493
Northwest Territories	$26,144	$89,562	$197,187	$304,812	$412,437
Yukon	$26,658	$89,106	$195,106	$301,106	$407,106
Nunavut	$24,158	$83,465	$184,715	$285,965	$387,215

One thing this table tells us is that the best way to minimize tax on the registered assets in your estate is to be a resident of Alberta or Nunavut when you die. Try to avoid dying in Quebec or Nova Scotia, both of which really sock it to the dearly departed.

Even on a relatively modest $100,000 RRIF (taxable income), the heirs of a deceased Quebecer will inherit $8461 less than those of someone who dies in Nunavut. On large estates, the tax gap becomes tens of thousands of dollars. The heirs of a Nova Scotia resident with a million-dollar RRIF will end up with $88,700 less than the survivors of a person who passes away in Alberta leaving behind the same amount. So anyone from the East Coast who left home to work in the oil fields won't do his family any favours by going back to Nova Scotia to die.

TFSAs and Estate Planning

The creation of TFSAs changes the estate-planning ground rules. That's because money accumulated in these plans does not attract any tax at death.

Therefore, one of the first priorities of older people who want to maximize the after-tax value of their estates should be to move as much money as possible from non-registered investment accounts into TFSAs.

For example, let's assume two spouses who are both 70 years old have $50,000 invested in non-registered accounts. Of this, $30,000 is in the wife's name and is invested in blue-chip stocks. The husband has the other $20,000 invested in GICs. They have two children to whom they want to leave equal shares of the estate. Neither spouse has opened a TFSA yet.

Looking at this situation strictly from an estate-planning perspective, the GICs will attract little tax at death, since they have no capital gains potential. Only the interest earned will be taxed. The stocks are another matter. The wife's portfolio took a beating in the market collapse of 2008–2009 and every stock in it is still in a loss position. However, she expects the stocks to move back into profit territory as the economy recovers. How should they proceed?

First, they should both open TFSAs immediately. They each have $10,000 in contribution room: $5000 for 2010 and $5000 carried forward from last year. Next, the wife should sell $20,000 worth of her money-losing securities. With the proceeds, she should contribute $10,000 to her own TFSA and give her husband the other $10,000 for his plan. Remember, it is important that she not contribute the losing stocks directly to a TFSA. If she makes a contribution in kind, the loss will not be allowed for tax purposes (but any capital gain triggered in such circumstances will be taxable). By selling them in the market, though, she crystallizes a capital loss that can be deducted from past, current, or future capital gains.

From a purely tax-planning perspective, this is not necessarily the best course of action because the interest earned on the husband's GIC is taxed at his marginal rate, whereas dividends and capital gains get a break. But the point of this exercise is to protect the children's inheritance from the taxman. If the couple uses the cash in the TFSAs to buy new stocks that appreciate in value, the capital gains will not be taxed when they die.

The couple should repeat this process each year until all of the wife's assets have been moved into the TFSAs. After that, the husband's GIC assets can be switched over in the same way. The GICs do not have to be sold first; they can go into the TFSA directly as a contribution in kind. Assuming they begin the process in 2010, by 2013, the couple's entire non-registered portfolio will be safe from taxation when they die.

Warning: Do not sell losing stocks in a non-registered account and buy them back immediately inside a TFSA. That would trigger what is technically known as the "superficial loss rule," meaning the Canada Revenue Agency would not recognize your capital loss for tax purposes. You must wait 30 days before repurchasing the same stock. However, you can buy shares in a different company any time.

RRSP/RRIF Strategies

A similar strategy could be considered with RRSPs and RRIFs, although the fact that any money withdrawn from these plans is taxable immediately makes the decision more complicated. In this situation, the current tax status of the plan holder is a major factor. If the person is in a low tax bracket, taking out an after-tax amount of $5000 a year and moving it into a TFSA may reduce the total tax bite on those savings at death. Let's look at the case of a B.C. man who is 70 years old and has $100,000 in a RRIF. He is a widower and plans to leave his estate to his only daughter. His annual taxable income is $32,000, which means his marginal tax rate is 20.06 percent (2009 rates). If he were to die at the end of this year, the $100,000 in the RRIF would be added to his income, increasing the total to $132,000 for purposes of his final tax return. The extra tax on the RRIF money would add $34,556 to the assessment, a tax rate of 34.56 percent. So his daughter would inherit only $65,444 of the proceeds of the RRIF after tax.

If the father withdraws an extra $6350 from his RRIF this year, he will be assessed $1343 tax on the payment (an effective rate of 21.1 percent), leaving him with just over $5000 after tax. He can then open a TFSA and deposit the money, repeating the same process each year. Essentially, he is paying tax at a much lower rate now than would be assessed on the RRIF if he dies. After the money goes into the TFSA, it grows tax-free, and no tax will be assessed on the plan's value at the time of his death.

This strategy is not a guaranteed financial winner because if the father lives long enough, the value of the RRIF may be reduced to the point where the tax assessed at death will be very low anyway. Moreover, by paying tax on the extra withdrawals early, he loses the investment income that this tax money could have earned if it had remained in the RRIF. Over five years, assuming annual compounding of 6 percent, $1343 will generate about $450 in investment income.

Although it does not apply in this illustration, people 65 or older with higher income need to consider whether extra RRIF or RRSP withdrawals will push them over the Old Age Security clawback threshold, thereby raising their effective tax rate. That would change the entire equation.

You will need to carefully analyze your particular situation before you take any action. If there is a large amount of money involved, consult a financial professional before embarking on this strategy.

Mass Confusion

TFSA succession planning has turned out to be something of a minefield. The reason: divided federal and provincial jurisdictions that resulted in unnecessary confusion and frustration for many account holders in the first half of 2009 and are still the source of legal debates over the precise meaning of certain terms.

It all started when Ottawa announced that as part of the TFSA program, anyone opening a plan could designate his or her spouse/partner as the "successor account holder." Successor holders would receive all the assets in the TFSA if the plan holder died. As a result, successors could withdraw the money tax-free or continue to manage the plan if they wished.

The problem is that succession laws are a provincial responsibility. Ottawa can say what it likes on the matter, but nothing actually happens in the real world until the provinces (and the territories) take action.

In most parts of Canada, that had not happened by the time TFSAs were launched at the beginning of 2009. Only a handful of provinces had passed legislation to allow successor holders to be named (and not by that specific term). The rest dragged their heels, in some cases until mid-year. There was no excuse for this delay; in most cases, the provinces simply added Tax-Free Savings Accounts to the list of registered plans that were permitted to transfer assets outside of probate.

(Quebec, which has a different set of laws under the Civil Code, never took action to allow for successor holders and never will; residents of that province must name a beneficiary in their will.)

The result was widespread uncertainty when the plans were launched. Residents of some provinces were allowed to make successor holder designations as part of their TFSA application. But in most regions, including populous Ontario, they were not. Since I had urged readers to name a successor account holder in my book *Tax-Free Savings Accounts*, I received numerous emails from unhappy people saying that their bank would not allow this and asking what to do.

Mea culpa. The book was written in September 2008, and at the time I assumed, incorrectly as it turned out, that the provinces would be onside by the time TFSAs were available. After all, they had been given almost a year's notice. As it turned out, only British Columbia, Alberta, Nova Scotia, New Brunswick, and Prince Edward Island were ready to go. The rest slowly signed on in the months that followed. Ontario was the last of the stragglers, implementing its succession law changes on June 16, five days after Manitoba. Now that the process is complete, every couple in Canada, outside Quebec, can name a successor holder and probate fees should not apply to TFSA transfers on death, although the provinces can make their own rules in this regard.

The practical effect of this provincial tardiness is that anyone who was unable to name a successor holder when they opened an account must now go back to the plan administrator and complete the required form. I strongly advise doing this, as it will make the whole transfer process much easier if anything should happen to you. Anyone opening a new account should be able to do this without difficulty.

That said, there is still some confusion about the difference between a successor account holder and a beneficiary. You need to understand the distinction because you may have both a successor holder form and a beneficiary form handed to you when you open an account.

To be clear, a successor holder can only be the spouse or common-law partner of the person who owns the TFSA. (Common-law partners must have lived together for at least three years or have children together.) No one else qualifies. The successor holder will take control of the TFSA when the original account holder dies, which means he or she can manage the assets in the plan and may make new contributions after an exemption period once it is transferred to his or her name. However, successor holders do not inherit any unused contribution room from the deceased. Any new contributions will be deducted from their personal limit. The successor holder can also make a new beneficiary designation and may cash out the plan at any time, tax-free.

A beneficiary is anyone else who is named to inherit a plan's assets: a child, sibling, relative, friend, or charity. A beneficiary will receive the assets of a TFSA, tax-free, at death, and the plan will be terminated. However, any profits earned within the TFSA between the time the holder dies and the date it is wound up will be taxable in the hands of the beneficiary.

Tax experts warn not to name your spouse/partner as a beneficiary but rather to use the successor holder designation. If you make a mistake and name the spouse as a beneficiary, the CRA will probably interpret that as meaning successor holder, but why risk complicating matters?

Don't name your spouse and someone else as joint beneficiaries. If you do, the rules of the game change and the transfer of assets will become more complicated because the spouse will no longer qualify as a successor holder.

In general, the rules governing the tax treatment of TFSAs after death are similar to those for RRSPs. TFSAs will retain their tax-exempt status until the end of the year following the year of the plan holder's death. So if a TFSA investor dies during 2011, the plan will keep its tax-exempt status until December 31, 2012. After that, it loses its TFSA status and becomes a plain, non-registered investment account. If that happens, every security in the portfolio will be assigned a fair market value, and any interest, dividends, or capital gains earned after that will be taxed at normal rates.

Let's consider some of the scenarios that can arise on the death of a TFSA plan holder.

1. The spouse or partner is named as the successor holder. In this case, the deceased person's TFSA can be continued or the assets can be withdrawn tax-free. The survivor retains his or her own TFSA and the contribution room he or she previously had. In effect, the successor holder simply steps into the shoes of the deceased.

2. The last surviving spouse or partner dies and the TFSA assets are divided between two children, an adult brother and sister.

In this case, the money in the plan at the time of death remains tax-free. However, any profits earned after death are taxable as income in their hands.

But here is an angle that will likely become increasingly important in estate planning. The executor has the flexibility to decide how the TFSA assets are divided and can use that discretion to minimize the tax due.

Let's assume that the TFSA had $100,000 in assets at the time of the plan holder's death and generated another $20,000 in gains before the estate was settled. In this case, the brother is unemployed and therefore has very little income. The sister is a vice-president of a large company and is in the top tax bracket. As the legislation is currently worded, the executor can direct that the sister's share of the $120,000 in the TFSA be received as a $60,000 tax-exempt transfer. The brother receives $40,000 in tax-exempt money and $20,000 in taxable income. Since he is in a very low bracket, the amount of tax he will actually end up paying will be minimal. (This is a loophole that may be closed in the future, so estate planners will need to keep watch on the situation.)

3. The status of the TFSA is not resolved by the end of the year following death. This will be a rare occurrence, but if it happens, the rules state that the TFSA becomes a taxable trust. The money that was in the plan at the time of death retains tax-exempt status. Any gains earned in the plan after death become taxable at trust rates. This status will continue until such time as the trust is liquidated.

Action Summary

1. Move assets from non-registered accounts into TFSAs to reduce tax at death.
2. Begin with securities that are likely to appreciate most in value.
3. Consult a financial professional before deciding whether to make early withdrawals from an RRSP or RRIF in order to make TFSA contributions.
4. Unless you live in Quebec, name your spouse or partner as the successor account holder when you open a TFSA. There is no standardized form for setting up a TFSA so be sure to review the application carefully. Make sure that it allows you to designate a successor holder. If it does not, ask if there is a separate form for this purpose.
5. Quebec residents should designate the person who is to receive the TFSA assets in their wills.
6. When TFSA assets pass to the next generation, the executor of the estate should ensure they are distributed in the most tax-efficient manner.

11

Tax-Saving Strategies

As we have already seen, there are many ways to save taxes by using TFSAs. However, we have only scratched the surface. Astute accountants and financial planners are continually coming up with more ideas, although some may be complex.

In this chapter, let's look at some easy-to-implement tax-saving strategies that we have not yet examined in depth.

Choose the Right Securities

In order to maximize the tax efficiency of your TFSA, it is essential you choose the right securities for the plan. If you're earning a return of only 0.75 percent, which is what Canada Savings Bonds were paying in the spring of 2009, it's hardly worth the effort to open a plan.

With RRSPs, the conventional wisdom is to hold interest-paying securities, such as bonds and GICs, inside the registered plan while keeping dividend-paying investments and growth stocks in a non-registered account. The logic for this is simple. All income drawn from an RRSP (or a RRIF/LIF) is taxed at your marginal rate, regardless of its original source. This means that interest, dividends, capital gains, and even return of capital are all taxed exactly the same when the money is earned inside a registered plan.

In the real world of non-registered accounts, the tax treatment is much different. Dividends are eligible for the dividend tax credit, which dramatically cuts the rate you actually pay. For example, a Saskatchewan resident with taxable income of $45,000 pays a marginal rate of 35 percent on RRSP or RRIF withdrawals. But the tax rate on dividends from public companies received in a non-registered account is only 7.3 percent. Clearly, it makes sense in this particular case to keep those dividend-paying stocks outside an RRSP if at all possible.

The same is true of any investments that have been purchased with a view to generating capital gains, such as stocks and equity mutual funds. If these securities are held in a non-registered account, only 50 percent of any gain is taxable, and gains can be offset by capital losses. But all capital gains earned in RRSPs and RRIFs will be taxed at your marginal rate when they come out and, to make matters worse, you can't claim any capital losses.

Certain types of securities also produce what is known as return of capital (ROC), which is not taxable in the year it is received. Income that is deemed to be ROC is deducted from the price you originally paid for the security, creating what is called an adjusted cost base (ACB). The ACB is eventually used to calculate any capital gain or loss when the security is sold. The net effect is that you benefit from tax sheltering until you sell, at which time you are taxed at the capital gains rate.[1]

A number of mutual fund companies offer products that make some or all of their distributions in the form of return of capital. But if you hold these inside an RRSP, all this clever tax-saving manipulation is lost.

TFSAs require a change in thinking. Since no taxes are assessed when money comes out of the plan, the RRSP tax planning strategies don't apply. You need to take a different approach if you are going to maximize the tax-free effectiveness of a TFSA.

A Capital Gains Strategy

In their 2006 campaign platform, the federal Conservatives promised to exempt capital gains from tax if the proceeds were reinvested within six months. They never delivered on that pledge, but TFSAs could have the long-term effect of making most capital gains tax-free. (There will be exceptions, such as a vacation property, as direct ownership of real estate within these plans is not permitted.)

So while it is true that capital gains receive a good break when they are earned outside a registered plan, they get even better treatment within a TFSA. Instead of paying tax on half of your profits, you get to keep the whole amount. The only downside is that you can't deduct capital losses incurred within a TFSA against gains made outside a plan.

Focusing a TFSA on capital gains looks even more attractive when we take another look at the contribution rules. Remember that any withdrawals from a plan are added back to your contribution limit in future years. So if you are smart or lucky (or both), you may be able to build your TFSA much faster than you might expect.

Let's consider a scenario that, while hypothetical, is certainly feasible. In the fall and winter of 2008–2009, world stock markets crashed. The S&P/TSX Composite Index lost more than 50 percent from its all-time high in early June 2008 to its low point in March 2009. It then shifted gears and staged a dramatic comeback, gaining more than 45 percent from March to

September. This is not unusual; we have seen similar patterns many times before.

The high-tech collapse that opened this century provides a good example. Between the late winter of 2000 and October 2002, stock markets dived, led down by NASDAQ, which eventually lost about 80 percent of its value. But after a final huge sell-off in September and October 2002 (technically known as the "capitulation" stage in a market collapse), a rally began. Between December 31, 2002, and June 6, 2008, the S&P/TSX Composite Index rose from 8221 to 15,155—a gain of 84 percent.

Many blue-chip stocks doubled, tripled, even quadrupled in value during that period. At one point during the 2002 sell-off, you could have bought shares in TD Bank for as low as $25.17. In November 2007, you could have sold them for as much as $75, a profit of almost 200 percent.

Resource stocks fared even better. The shares of Potash Corporation of Saskatchewan traded as low as $13.23 during 2002. In June 2008, they touched a high of $246.29—an astounding gain of more than 1700 percent!

It's unrealistic to expect to pick winners of that magnitude on a consistent basis. What is *not* unrealistic is the possibility—indeed the probability—that high-quality stocks will double in value in the two to three years following the end of a deep bear market.

Here is a capital gains strategy that flows from that thinking. If you have not already done so, open a TFSA now and invest the $5000 yearly contribution limit plus any carry-forward room you have accumulated in two or three quality stocks. Choose companies that are industry leaders and have a well-established history of surviving even the toughest times.

Let's assume you invest a total of $10,000. You select the stocks carefully and buy when prices are relatively cheap. If the scenario plays out as predicted, by the end of the second year, your TFSA stands a good chance of doubling in value. You now have $20,000 in the plan. You decide to sell the stocks and withdraw the cash to use for the down payment on a rental property. There are no capital gains taxes to pay.

In the next year, your contribution room will increase to $25,000—the $5000 basic entitlement plus the $20,000 you withdrew. Now you can begin the process of rebuilding the TFSA to the extent that your financial resources permit. The net result is that you now own an income property plus you have increased the amount of money you can shelter from tax in the future.

Of course, the timing has to be right, you must have the temperament to accept stock market risk, and you must choose the right companies for this to work. But it is a strategy worth considering, especially coming out of a bear market.

A Dividend Strategy

At first glance, it would seem that the capital gains strategy I have described would also apply to dividends. Yes, they get a tax advantage in a non-registered account, but you pay no tax at all if they are earned in a TFSA.

But here's the wrinkle. If your taxable income is relatively low and you invest in dividend stocks with little or no growth potential (preferred shares are a classic example), you may decide to use the TFSA for something else.

There are some quirks to the dividend tax credit that require close examination before you make a decision. Let's look at the situation of a 75-year-old widowed grandmother who lives with her children in Ontario. She has a small pension, which, when added to her CPP and OAS payments, gives her taxable income of

$25,000 a year. She has recently inherited a modest investment portfolio from her husband, which consists almost entirely of bank preferred shares. The dividends from the portfolio will add $3000 a year to her income.

In this case, there is no tax advantage to putting the preferred shares into a TFSA (assuming they will never generate a capital gain). That's because at her income level, the effect of the dividend tax credit will be to reduce the tax payable on the investment income to zero. (This would also be the case in every province except Quebec and New Brunswick.)

Compare her situation with that of a Quebec-based senior vice-president of a large public corporation who owns 100,000 shares of the company's common stock and has taxable income of $85,000. In his case, the dividends will be taxed at a rate of 26.06 percent (2009 rates). He should contribute $5000 worth of his shares to a TFSA every year and give his wife $5000 worth to do the same.

There is also another circumstance in which dividend-paying securities should be considered for TFSA accounts. That's when a taxpayer is vulnerable to the Old Age Security clawback. I'll explain this in more detail later in this chapter.

An Interest Strategy

Although interest income is taxed at your marginal rate, the tax-saving potential of a TFSA for GICs, Canada Savings Bonds (CSBs), and so forth is limited, especially at a time when rates are low. For example, if you invested $5000 in the P69 issue of Canada Premium Bonds, which came out in April 2009, the total amount of tax-sheltered income you will receive over the first three years will be only $236. That's less than $80 a year! With returns like that, it's hardly worthwhile to set up a plan.

Still, many people prefer the safety of interest-bearing securities to the risk of stock market investing. For those who have a long time horizon, there is certainly an advantage in using a TFSA for this purpose instead of leaving the money in a taxable account. The key is to aim for the highest possible return, consistent with safety.

In the summer of 2009, for example, several financial institutions were offering five-year GICs with a yield of 3.85 percent. If you had invested $5000 and tax-sheltered the interest in a TFSA, you would have earned $1040 in tax-free profit at maturity.

Avoiding the Dreaded Clawback

One of the most contentious tax laws on the books is the clawback of Old Age Security payments from those Canadians age 65 and older who are deemed to be in the "high-income" category. For the 2009 tax year, the threshold that pushed people into this class was net income exceeding $66,335 (the figure increases annually in line with inflation).

The tax is a stiff one: a 15 percent surcharge on every dollar of net income above the limit until the entire OAS payment has been recovered. For a Manitoba resident with taxable income of $70,000, the effect is to increase the marginal tax rate on the affected portion of her income to 54.4 percent.

Obviously, OAS recipients who are close to the threshold are motivated to do anything they can to stay below it. TFSAs provide two new ways to achieve this.

The first derives from the fact that TFSA withdrawals are not considered to be taxable income, unlike RRSP withdrawals or RRIF payments. This isn't a significant factor now, but as time goes on and TFSA balances increase, people who are close to the threshold will be able to draw cash from the plans without risking having their OAS payments clawed back.

The second way in which TFSAs can be used to reduce or eliminate exposure to the clawback is more subtle. It involves using the plans to circumvent what I regard as one of the most unfair aspects of the Income Tax Act, but one that no government seems willing to change.

We have already looked at the advantages of the dividend tax credit. But the credit can be a double-edged sword when it comes to the OAS clawback. That is because of the way it is calculated and the structure of the income tax return.

There is nothing simple about the dividend tax credit. Calculating it is a two-stage operation. The first involves a "gross-up" of the actual dividend income you receive to what is technically called the "taxable amount of dividends." The second step is to multiply that number by a percentage factor to arrive at the actual amount you can deduct from your income tax. For what the government classifies as "eligible dividends," which includes all public companies, that factor is 18 percent for the 2010 tax year. For dividends that are not deemed eligible (typically those from private companies), the factor is 13.3333 percent.[2] As I said, this is not simple!

Here is the problem as it relates to the clawback. The grossed-up amount of dividends received is used to calculate net income. (This is unlike the treatment accorded to capital gains, where only half the profit is included in the net income calculation.) The result is that people who receive dividends run the risk of incurring tax on money that they never actually received—I call it "phantom income."

It works like this. Every dollar of eligible dividend income you collect is grossed up by 44 percent in 2010. So, for purposes of calculating exposure to the OAS clawback, $1.00 of income is treated as if you had actually received $1.44. (In 2011, the gross-up will decline to 41 percent and in 2012 it will be 38 percent). Clearly, people who depend on dividends for a significant portion of their retirement income could find themselves pushed over the clawback threshold as a result.

This is not a theoretical exercise. Low interest rates and the demise of income trusts have forced many older people to look for other investments that will provide them with the cash flow they need to live on. As it happens, the big banks came out with new issues of high-yielding preferred shares in 2008 and early 2009 as a way to increase their capital base (Tier 1 capital, as it is technically known). These preferreds offered dividend yields as high as 6.5 percent, which would be equivalent to more than 9 percent from a bond in after-tax terms.

The trap is the gross-up. Someone who receives $15,000 in eligible dividends in 2010 will have to declare $21,600 as net income, which could be enough to move her into clawback territory.

You can use TFSAs to alleviate this dilemma. By using the plans to invest in preferred shares (or dividend-paying common stocks), you'll lose the dividend tax credit, but you also avoid the gross-up problem. This strategy isn't applicable to everyone, but it should be considered by those who have invested (or want to invest) in dividend-paying securities and who have income that brings them close to the OAS threshold.

Inheritance Shelters

The next 10 to 20 years will see an intergenerational transfer of billions of dollars in personal wealth. As the money passes from parents to children, the issue will be how to manage the transfer in a tax-effective way.

As explained in Chapter 10, the money in a TFSA at the time of the death of the last surviving spouse will pass to the next generation tax-free, unlike RRSP/RRIF assets that will be taxed at the decedent's marginal rate. After that, if any portion of the money is invested, the profits are subject to tax at the applicable rates.

So TFSAs offer an efficient way to shelter part or all of an inheritance from future taxes. By 2013, for example, an older couple who have not made any TFSA investments will have $52,000 in available contribution room, as shown in the table in Chapter 3. By 2018, this will have increased to $109,000.

Although this may not be enough to shelter the full amount of an inheritance, it will certainly help to reduce the tax bite when they die if they move as much money as possible into TFSAs.

If the couple combines this approach with another tax-avoidance technique, such as paying off any existing mortgage on their tax-free principal residence, the proceeds from all but the largest estates may eventually end up being tax-exempt when the parents pass on.

The same principle applies to lottery winnings, should you be so lucky.

Investment Loans

It's against the law to use an RRSP as collateral for a loan. That is not the case with a TFSA. The money in a TFSA can be used as security if you need to borrow cash for any reason. This loan can be for any purpose, from obtaining emergency funds to adding to your investments.

To illustrate, let's assume that you have accumulated $10,000 in a TFSA and invested the money in five-year GICs. Unless you have chosen redeemable GICs, that cash is locked in until maturity.

Suddenly, you are laid off and you need the money. You can't cash in the GICs, but you can go to the bank and ask them for a loan, using the assets of your TFSA as collateral. Since the money in the plan is in guaranteed certificates, there should be no problem obtaining the temporary cash you need.

Another possibility, and one that will probably be promoted by financial advisers during periods when stock markets are rising, is to use the money in a TFSA to leverage your investment portfolio. Because of the risks involved, this is not a strategy I recommend except for very knowledgeable investors, but if you know what you are doing, it is a way to potentially increase profits. (It's also a way to increase losses, as people who had borrowed to invest learned to their dismay in the crash of 2008–2009.)

To illustrate this situation, let's look five years down the road. You've been contributing the maximum amount to a TFSA every year and, with the earnings on the invested money, your plan has a value of $35,000. The entire amount is held in a diversified portfolio of mutual funds.

You decide to use the TFSA as collateral to borrow additional money to invest. Since the mutual funds are not guaranteed, the bank won't offer a loan equal to the full value of the plan, but it agrees to advance you $20,000 at prime. You invest the money in a non-registered portfolio of mutual funds, bringing the total amount of your assets to $55,000.

Over the next five years, your investments earn an average of 7 percent annually. Some of that return will be tax-sheltered by the TFSA, but the money earned on the non-registered portfolio will be taxable. At the end of that time, the original $35,000 in the TFSA will have increased to $49,089. Assuming an average tax rate of 25 percent on the non-registered portfolio, the $20,000 you invested there will be worth $25,831.

However, you need to subtract the interest cost of the loan from your return. As is the case with RRSP loans, you cannot deduct the interest expense on a TFSA loan for tax purposes, so you are on the hook for the full amount. For purposes of this illustration, let's assume the interest cost reduces your net after-tax profit by half. Your actual gain on the borrowed $20,000 after five years is $2916.

(In their booklet on Tax-Free Savings Accounts, the Tax and Estate Planning team at Mackenzie Financial suggests that you can make the interest deductible by transferring assets from a non-registered portfolio to a TFSA. "Your non-registered assets could then be repurchased with borrowed funds," the team says. "In this case, a direct link from the borrowed money to an eligible non-registered investment would be established, and interest should be tax-deductible."[3])

At this point, you repay the bank loan and pocket the money. The end result is that you have completed the transaction with a total gain of just over $18,000. Since you had only $35,000 of your own money at risk (the rest came from the bank), your return on investment for the period is 51.4 percent. That works out to 8.65 percent annually. The bottom line is that you have improved your average annual compound rate of return (which was nominally 7 percent) by almost one-quarter through leveraging.

Of course, the higher the rate of return you earn, the greater the impact of leveraging. But the risk quotient also increases. This is why I stress again that only experienced investors should consider this strategy.

Action Summary

1. Give careful thought to the securities you hold in your TFSA, with a view to maximizing tax effectiveness.

2. Be sure you understand the differences between the tax-planning guidelines for RRSPs and RRIFs and those for TFSAs.

3. Focusing a TFSA on capital gains has the potential of producing large profits quickly, especially coming out of a bear market. Beware of the increased risk in this approach.

4. Do not automatically invest in dividend-paying stocks within a TFSA, especially those with little or no capital gains potential, such as preferred shares. This is especially important for lower-income people. Examine the tax implications carefully before deciding.

5. If you use a TFSA to hold interest-bearing securities such as bonds or GICs, look for the highest return consistent with safety.

6. The "gross-up" applied to dividends can result in some people who collect Old Age Security being pushed into an extremely high tax bracket on the basis of money they never actually receive. Anyone in this position should consider putting dividend-paying stocks in a TFSA if you are at risk.

7. Use TFSAs to shelter intergenerational inheritances from tax.

8. TFSAs can be used as collateral for a loan, although the interest is not tax-deductible. If—and only if—you are experienced and knowledgeable, you can take advantage of this to increase the size of your investment portfolio through leveraging.

12

Special Situations

After the launch of *Tax-Free Savings Accounts* in January 2009, I received hundreds of questions from people who were trying to understand the ins and outs of this new investment opportunity.

One came from a woman who asked whether she would earn more profit by moving her money from a U.S. index fund to a TFSA. "I am not really sure which is the better investment," she wrote.

In my reply, I explained that the two were not mutually exclusive. Think of a TFSA as an empty box, I suggested. You can fill it with any kind of investments you want, provided you have the right type of plan and they qualify under the guidelines of the Canada Revenue Agency. So, if she wished to do so, she could open a self-directed TFSA and transfer the U.S. index fund directly into it, up to the contribution limit.

After she received my reply, she wrote back, "Thank you for your response. It appears there is more to this than just dumping $5000 into a TFSA."

Yes, there certainly is, which is why this book was written. And with each passing month the complexities surrounding TFSAs become more apparent. In this chapter, I'll look at some of the special situations that have emerged thus far.

U.S. Dividends

Several years ago, Canada and the United States reached an agreement to recognize and respect the integrity of the tax-sheltered retirement savings plans available in each country. This understanding was subsequently formalized as part of the Canada–U.S. Tax Treaty.

Under the terms of the agreement, dividends paid by American corporations into Canadian retirement plans such as RRSPs and RRIFs are exempt from the 15 percent withholding tax that applies to payments made to non-registered accounts. Americans receive the same treatment for Canadian dividends paid into IRAs, 401(k) plans, and so on.

However, TFSAs are not covered by the tax treaty and may never be, as they are not considered to be "retirement accounts"—the money can be used for any purpose. Therefore, the exemption from U.S. withholding tax does not apply to dividends paid to your TFSA. As a result, your plan will receive only 85 percent of any dividend declared by an American company whose stock you own.

That's not the only financial penalty for putting U.S. stocks into a TFSA. In the case of non-registered accounts, investors can recover part or all of the 15 percent withholding tax by claiming a foreign tax credit when they file their Canadian returns. That credit is not available when the dividend is paid to a TFSA because the income is tax-sheltered. The bottom line is that the investor is out of luck as far as the tax people are concerned.

This creates a disincentive for holding U.S. dividend-paying stocks in a TFSA. However, don't write them off entirely because there is another way to look at this. If you receive U.S. dividends outside a TFSA, they will be taxed at your marginal rate (non-Canadian dividends are not eligible for the dividend tax credit). That means you could pay tax at a rate as high as 48.25 percent depending on where you live and your total income. Inside a TFSA, the dividends will be taxed at only a 15 percent rate—the U.S. withholding tax.

That actually may be a better deal than holding the U.S. shares in an RRSP or RRIF, and that's because withdrawals from those plans are taxed at your marginal rate. So, while you avoid the withholding tax at the time of the payments, you'll be hit when the dividends come out, probably at a higher rate than 15 percent.

Don't automatically exclude U.S. stocks from your TFSA. Just be sure you understand that, in this particular situation, any profits will not be entirely tax-free.

Moving Abroad

Just because Canada recognizes a particular plan as a tax shelter does not mean that another country will. So, if you are considering taking up residence abroad, you need to give some thought to your TFSA and what to do about it.

Only Canadian residents can contribute to a TFSA. But if you already have a plan and move elsewhere, you are allowed to keep it and to make withdrawals from it. As far as this country is concerned, any such withdrawals will continue to be tax-free. But your new host country may not be so generous.

For example, if you move to the United States, the Internal Revenue Service (IRS) will recognize assets in an RRSP or RRIF at the time you take up residence there as capital and therefore not taxable. Plus any income earned within the plan after you become a U.S. resident may continue to compound tax-free. You only become liable for U.S. taxes once you start making withdrawals and then only on those amounts that relate to income earned in your RRSP or RRIF after you became a U.S. resident, plus any unrealized capital gains.

(This makes it a sound strategy to take any capital gains in your RRSP before you leave Canada, thereby reducing the U.S. tax for which you'll eventually be liable. If you've lost money in your RRSP to the extent that the plan's value is less than your total contributions, you'll face no U.S. tax at all.)

You will have to pay a withholding tax of 25 percent in Canada when you make withdrawals from your RRSP after you become a non-resident by moving to the United States. Periodic payments from a RRIF, LIF, or annuity are subject to a 15 percent withholding tax. (Withholding rates may differ if you move to another country; the standard rate on pensions, RRIFs, and annuities is 25 percent, but any tax treaty provisions take precedence.)

Those are the RRSP/RRIF rules. However, because TFSAs are so new there are no formal arrangements in place for dealing with them. At this point, no one can say with certainty how they will be dealt with by local tax authorities. There has been a great deal of discussion among Canadian tax experts on how the United States might treat TFSAs, based on the principles contained in the Canada–U.S. Tax Treaty. As for other countries, no one I spoke to wanted to venture an opinion. "We don't have enough information for other countries yet," said Sandy Cardy, vice-president of Tax and Estate Planning Service for Mackenzie Financial.

Gena Katz, executive director, Tax Practice, with the accounting firm of Ernst & Young, says that withdrawals from a TFSA after a Canadian takes up residence in the United States would not be taxable because the amounts are considered capital. "Either they represent pre-resident capital or income that has been taxed in U.S. and is now capital," she wrote in an email response to a question.

However, Cardy warns that there may be an exception in the case of securities with unrealized capital gains that are sold after U.S. residency is established. "Capital gains realized at the time of sale would likely be taxed on withdrawal," she said. "My understanding is that income earned annually would not be taxed on withdrawal as it is taxed in the year it is earned. Clients might want to bump up their ACB [adjusted cost base] before leaving Canada to reduce tax payable in the U.S. on unrealized capital gains."

Clearly, you need to tread very carefully if you find yourself in this situation.

There is another potential problem. Canadian brokers who are not registered in the United States (which is most of them) cannot make trades in your account once you become a non-resident. Even those who are registered are limited in what they are allowed to do. State regulations make matters even more complicated. So, before you leave Canada to take up permanent residency elsewhere, make sure you sit down with your financial adviser and discuss exactly what the status of your TFSA will be after you depart in terms of your ability to make trades (ask the same question if you have a RRIF or an RRSP). If the account will be frozen, you may decide to close it before you leave. If there is a lot of money involved, this is a major decision, so explore all the options thoroughly.

If no one can give you definitive answers to these issues before you emigrate (and that is very likely), you should consider the pros and cons of terminating the plan and withdrawing the money while you are still a Canadian resident. By doing so, you know for sure that no tax will be assessed.

Jamie Golombek, managing director, Tax and Estate Planning for CIBC Private Wealth Management, says that the tax advantages of keeping the account after emigrating would mostly be lost since it is unlikely the country you are moving to will recognize the tax-free status of the TFSA. "Presumably, a country like the United States would treat a TFSA as a regular investment account or possibly as an offshore trust," he said. "If you are going to leave Canada permanently, while not necessary, you may wish to cash out the TFSA before you go. If you withdraw the money before you become a resident of another country, you know it won't be taxed (unless you're a U.S. citizen). There is no such assurance once you leave."

Katz agrees: "Unless there is tax relief, there is no benefit to keeping a TFSA if an individual will become a permanent non-resident."

Cardy says there may be some special situations in which keeping the TFSA makes sense: "Where the client might be able to benefit from leaving the plan in Canada is if they have U.S. foreign tax credits for foreign tax paid on foreign income. Where this is the case, the credits can be used to offset U.S. tax on the TFSA income even though the credits were not sourced from TFSA income."

She also notes that if you keep your TFSA after moving to the United States and the value of the plan exceeds US$10,000, you may need to file an FBAR form (Report of Foreign Banks and Financial Accounts) with the IRS. It is used to collect information on foreign plans to ensure tax and regulatory compliance.

I made an effort to get some indication from the IRS about how the United States views TFSAs. They wanted nothing to do with it. A call to Robert Marvin at the national media office was met with the instruction to send an email. The email was never answered.

After collecting all the available information, I came to the personal conclusion that I would cash in my TFSA if I ever decided to move to the United States. The hassles of keeping it outweigh the benefits as far as I'm concerned. But talk to a tax adviser before you take action because this is a very fluid situation.

Shares in Small Businesses

One of the fastest ways to build assets in a TFSA is to use a self-directed plan to hold shares of a small business with high growth potential. This is perfectly legal, but the rules are complex and you must be careful to adhere to them.

I received the following question from a reader who had managed to build the $5000 he contributed to his TFSA early in 2009 to $12,000 by August. Now he wanted to aim even higher.

I own shares in a private company (some held in a non-registered account, some in my RRSP). The company will be going public later this year. So I have three questions:

1) Is it possible to use cash in my TFSA to buy more shares in the private company (assuming I have the opportunity to buy more)?

2) If "no" to #1, is it possible to swap the private shares in my non-registered account for cash in my TFSA prior to the company getting publicly listed?

3) If "no" to #2, is it possible to swap the private shares in my non-registered account for cash in the TFSA the instant they

are publicly listed, and at the share price I paid rather than whatever the market value turns out to be that day or at close of day?

I've had conflicting information from my current broker, from CRA, and from articles I've read. I hope you can shed some light!

For starters, TFSAs use the same rules for holding small business shares as apply to RRSPs. In general, these allow a plan holder to invest in the stock of an active Canadian small business provided the contributor (or a plan beneficiary) is not a "connected shareholder."

(The CRA's definition of a connected shareholder is a person who owns 10 percent or more of the company's stock at the time the shares go into the registered plan unless the person deals at arm's length with the firm and the aggregate cost of all shares owned is not more than $25,000.)

Also, it must be clear that any profit on the stock does not represent a payment to the plan holder by the issuer of the shares.

The small business does not have to be publicly traded. It may be an active taxable Canadian corporation, a venture capital company, or a "specified holding company." However, it must qualify as "Canadian," which means that at least 50 percent of its full-time employees are in Canada or at least 50 percent of the salaries "are reasonably attributable to services provided in Canada."

So let's go back to the reader's questions with these facts in mind.

Yes, he can use the cash in his TFSA to buy shares in the private company, as long as it meets the eligibility tests and he is not a connected shareholder. However, the shares must be purchased at fair market value, which may not be easy to determine if the company does not trade publicly.

No, he cannot swap the private shares in his non-registered account for the cash in the TFSA, either before or after it goes public. Amendments to the Income Tax Act introduced in October 2009 prohibit this kind of transaction.

Obviously, this can be a tricky situation. If there is any doubt at all, I suggest obtaining professional advice before proceeding. The penalties for holding prohibited securities in a TFSA are severe, and swaps are now offside as well. And keep in mind that even though a particular manoeuvre may be legal, not all brokerage firms may be willing to execute it. Each company has its own policies and procedures so discuss the situation with the broker or a supervisor first.

Action Summary

1. Dividends from U.S. companies paid into a TFSA will be subject to a 15 percent withholding tax and there is no way to recover that money. So consider the situation carefully before you buy U.S. stocks for your portfolio.
2. If you plan to emigrate from Canada permanently, give serious consideration to cashing in your TFSA before you leave. There is no guarantee that your new country of residence will recognize the tax-free status of the plan.
3. Shares in a small business corporation are eligible for inclusion in a TFSA provided they meet CRA requirements. But they must be contributed or purchased at fair market value and cannot be swapped into a plan. Professional advice is recommended.

13

How to Invest

TFSAs are unlike any government-sanctioned savings plan we've seen before. All the others have a specific purpose: retirement planning, education savings, or building an account for a disabled person. By contrast, a TFSA can be used for anything.

It can be a source of emergency money. It can be used for saving to buy a home. It can be a supplementary retirement plan. It can be used to build a tax-sheltered estate. It can be a speculative investment account. Or it can be all of these at various times.

In short, a TFSA can be whatever you want it to be. You define the objectives and set the time frames. Then you decide how to invest the money so as to achieve your goals most effectively.

The fluid nature of a TFSA makes it impossible to establish specific investment guidelines that will be suitable to all plans. There are no "right" or "wrong" investments; it all depends on what you are trying to achieve. For example, someone looking to maximize capital gains within a plan would never even consider a money market fund. But for someone who wants a virtually risk-free source of ready cash to use in an emergency, a money fund may be a perfect fit.

This puts the onus on TFSA investors to choose the right type of plan and to think out their investment strategies very carefully before making decisions. Do not, under any circumstances, simply walk into a financial institution and say you want to open a TFSA. You could end up with a plan that is totally unsuited to your needs. Decide in advance what your primary investment goal will be and then select the type of plan that best suits your objective. Once that is done, choose investments that fit the strategy.

If your main goal is to build an emergency fund, see Chapter 5, "Rainy Day TFSAs," for suggestions on where to invest. Here are some ideas if you have different priorities.

Saving for a Home

As I pointed out in Chapter 6, your first choice if you are saving money to buy a home should be an RRSP. You can build your assets much more quickly because RRSPs have higher contribution limits than TFSAs. Once you have accumulated $25,000, you can borrow the money interest-free to use for a down payment on a house under the provisions of the popular Home Buyers' Plan (HBP).

However, you can use a TFSA to add to your house savings. And if you don't qualify for the HBP because you or your spouse has owned a home within a certain time frame, a TFSA is certainly a worthwhile alternative. (There are some other restrictions to the HBP as well; check the Home Buyers' Plan guide available on the Canada Revenue Agency website.)

If you use a TFSA, there are three important considerations in planning your investment strategy. The first is to decide how much money you want to have available for the down payment. The second is to set a target date for accumulating the money you need. The third is to determine an appropriate risk/reward trade-off.

In most cases, a long-term savings plan is not appropriate. People don't want to wait 20 years for a house. So we'll set the time frame at a maximum of five years.

As for how much you need to save, that's a mathematical calculation. For a conventional mortgage, you'll require at least 20 percent of the cost of the house as a down payment. So, if you are thinking in terms of a $300,000 home, you'll need $60,000. For a two-income couple, that's $30,000 each.

That's the easy part. Deciding on how much risk to accept is more difficult. One of the axioms of investing is the higher the potential return, the greater the risk involved. It's understandable that people want to save enough for a down payment as quickly as possible, but at what cost? Imagine the disappointment if you had been about ready to buy a home in mid-2008 and then saw half your savings wiped out in the market crash.

So let's do some calculations. Suppose you and your spouse/partner are starting to save for a house this year. You each plan to contribute $5000 annually to a TFSA for the next five years. What rate of return do you need to generate to have $30,000 in each plan at the end of that time?

The answer is 6.15 percent. You are unlikely to achieve that level of return by investing in a GIC and certainly not by holding the money in a savings account. However, a good balanced fund might do the job, providing there are no market meltdowns over the period. Balanced funds are normally relatively low risk, but even the most cautiously managed of them suffered in the 2008–2009 stock market dive.

If you don't like the risk, you have a choice: You can lower your expectations by starting with a less expensive home or you can extend your time frame by a year or two. Using our example, waiting one more year would mean $30,000 would have been contributed to both TFSAs. Any investment income earned would be a bonus so our fictional couple could put the money into safe GICs and protect themselves from unexpected loss. (They just need to be sure the GICs will have matured by the time they need the cash.)

Alternatively, they could decide to start with a $250,000 house. This would enable them to accumulate the needed down payment in five years while keeping the money in GICs.

The type of TFSA chosen will depend on the strategy used. If the decision is safety first, a GIC plan is a good choice. If you are willing to take more risk to earn a higher return, a mutual fund or self-directed plan is recommended.

Maximizing Profits

Many people will see TFSAs as an opportunity to score big tax-free investment gains. If you have a lot of investing experience and can handle the risk, you may be in that group. But keep your priorities straight. Pay off your debts and top up your RRSP before setting out to make a tax-sheltered fortune.

A "big hit" approach requires a self-directed plan that allows you to trade all types of TFSA-eligible securities. Since anyone who goes this route is presumably quite knowledgeable about the markets, a discount brokerage account is preferable because of the reduced costs.

There may be a temptation to focus on speculative penny stocks in your plan, but you can reduce the risk significantly by buying blue chips when they're cheap. For example, investors sold off Canadian banks in the winter of 2009 on fears of a global financial collapse. The prices fell so much that you could have bought shares of Bank of Montreal in March for just over $24. By August, they were trading at \$54.75 for a gain of 128 percent in only five months! We saw a similar phenomenon with energy shares, as well as with numerous other companies.

The best strategy in this situation is to buy a quality stock when the price is down and wait until it (hopefully) doubles. At that point take half-profits and buy something else. This will enable you to diversify your TFSA portfolio, thereby reducing risk.

Retirement Savings

If you want to use a TFSA as a retirement savings vehicle to supplement a pension plan and/or an RRSP, you should aim for a respectable rate of growth. However, you must be careful to avoid undue risk.

In this case, consider your TFSA as a personal pension plan. Now think about how professional money managers handle pension accounts. They are very conservative, and with good reason. These men and women have been entrusted with the retirement savings of all the contributors to the plan, who are depending on them to ensure that the money will be there when it comes time to draw on it. So the last thing they can afford is to take big risks that might result in heavy losses. Your TFSA should be handled the same way. Risk should be kept to a minimum and your securities should be chosen accordingly.

Over the years, I have seen a tendency in people to throw caution to the winds in their RRSP accounts and suffer the consequences for their recklessness. I believe there are two reasons for this. One is the fact that retirement seems a long way off, especially to anyone under 40. As a result, the assets in an RRSP take on a sort of Monopoly money aura. So taking some chances doesn't seem like a big deal. If things don't work out there will be no impact on the person's lifestyle, so why not roll the dice?

There is a danger that we will see the same attitude with some TFSAs. Money will be invested carelessly, with little thought given to the importance of capital preservation. Then another stock market collapse will occur such as we experienced in 2008–2009 and people will be bewailing the losses they have suffered and complaining that they have been forced to put their retirement plans on hold as a result. If you are counting on your TFSA to help you maintain your lifestyle when you stop work, don't make that mistake.

In my book *The Retirement Time Bomb*, I recommended that asset allocation within an RRSP be adjusted according to age, making the plan more conservative as the holder approaches retirement. The same formula could be applied to a retirement-savings TFSA. Here it is.

Asset Allocation by Age

Years	20–25	26–49	50–59	60–65	66+
Cash	5%	5%	5%	5%	10%
Fixed income	30%	20%	30%	40%	40%
Variable income	10%	10%	15%	20%	25%
Growth	55%	65%	50%	35%	25%

Cash includes currency and highly liquid cash-equivalent securities such as treasury bills, money market funds, and Canada Savings Bonds. Any asset that can quickly be converted to cash for its full face value qualifies.

Fixed-income securities pay a specified (fixed) rate of return and have a maturity date, at which time your principal is returned. Bonds, mortgages, fixed-rate preferred shares, and GICs fall into this asset class.

Variable-income securities offer cash flow on a predictable basis (usually monthly or quarterly), but the amount of the payment is not guaranteed and may vary considerably. These securities may or may not have a maturity date. Examples include floating-rate preferred shares, income mutual funds, some exchange-traded funds, and income trusts (although there may be few of those left after 2011).

Growth assets add value mainly through capital gains. Stocks and equity mutual funds are the most common examples.

Looking at the table, you'll see that for the 20 to 25 age group the income recommendation is higher than for those in the 26 to 49 range while the growth component is smaller. I believe younger people who are just starting out should take a balanced approach to investing until they have learned more about how securities perform and better understand the ins and outs of portfolio management. There is a danger—and I have seen it happen—that young people may tend to be somewhat aggressive with their initial investments. It's a risk I would advise you to avoid if you are serious about using a TFSA as a retirement-savings plan.

As a person becomes more comfortable with investing—and the ages shown here are only a broad guideline—the percentage of higher-risk variable income and growth securities in the plan can be increased. People in their late twenties, thirties, and even their forties can take a long-term view of the markets and not be overly concerned about temporary setbacks. However, I recommend that a portion of all portfolios be kept in fixed-income securities, both to mitigate risk and to take advantage of those occasions when bonds outperform stocks as they did in 2008 and early 2009.

As you approach your retirement years, you should gradually reduce the risk in your portfolio since the time left to ride out any severe stock market setback is running short. Build your cash and income components, which will be needed when the time comes to convert your savings to a revenue stream. However, I suggest you always retain a portion of your portfolio in growth securities as a protection against even modest rates of inflation. You don't want to outlive your money!

Suitable securities for a retirement-savings TFSA include money market funds, bonds, bond funds, GICs, preferred shares, balanced funds, conservatively managed large-cap equity funds, and carefully selected low-risk equities such as utility stocks. Avoid speculative stocks and high-volatility mutual funds and exchange-traded funds (ETFs).

Education Savings

Although an RESP is the best way to save for a child's education, some parents may wish to avoid the tax risk associated with those plans (see Chapter 8) or use a TFSA to put additional money aside.

If this is your main goal, the key to success is to reduce the investment risk in the plan as the child gets older. By the time he or she is ready to begin post-secondary education, the assets in the plan should be entirely in cash and fixed-income securities so as to ensure that the money for tuition, books, and so on will be available. There is nothing worse than scrimping and saving for years only to see it all wiped out by a stock market bust just as your youngster is ready to start university.

For education savings, I suggest using either a mutual fund plan or a self-directed TFSA. If the child is very young and the initial amount invested is small, begin with a conservatively managed, balanced fund. This will provide immediate diversification while keeping risk to a minimum. As the assets grow, you can add more funds to the account.

Let's assume you begin the process when the child is a baby and that you expect he or she will enter university at age 18. Here is how the asset mix could be adjusted as the child ages. (Note that I have dropped the variable-income line from this table, as it is not as relevant here.)

Asset Allocation by Age

Years	1–10	11–14	15–18	18+
Cash	5%	10%	15%	20%
Fixed income	20%	35%	60%	80%
Growth	75%	55%	25%	0%

The purpose of this approach is to maximize the growth potential of the plan in the early years. After age 10, the risk is reduced by cutting back on the growth weighting. Once the student enters university, all the assets should be in cash and fixed-income securities. This will preserve capital while ensuring that the money will be available to draw on as needed.

As for which securities to select, the same broad rules apply as for retirement savings.

Post-Retirement Income

TFSAs have opened a whole new world of investing opportunities for older people. Until they were introduced, there was no cheap and effective way to tax-shelter investment income after age 71, the year when RRSPs must be terminated. But there is no age limit for contributing to a TFSA so Canadians who have passed the RRSP cut-off and have some money to invest should take advantage of these plans.

Most people in this age group will have one of two goals. Either they will see a TFSA as a way to provide a tax-sheltered estate for their heirs or they will want to make periodic withdrawals from the plan to supplement their retirement income.

If generating tax-free income is the main objective, focus on low- to medium-risk securities that provide decent cash flow. Examples include high-grade corporate bonds (rated BBB or better), good quality preferred shares, conservative dividend-paying stocks (for example, utilities), some REITs, and monthly income mutual funds or ETFs. A self-directed TFSA is the best suited for this purpose.

If possible, don't make withdrawals from the TFSA for a few years to allow the capital to build to a respectable level. Once you begin drawing income, try to limit the annual amount to no more than the cash flow generated within the plan over the previous 12 months. That way, your capital will remain intact.

Estate Planning

If you are using a TFSA to build a tax-sheltered inheritance for your heirs, you probably want to provide maximum protection for the assets in the plan. At this stage in your life, growth is not the main objective and presumably you don't need additional income. Rather, you want to preserve the wealth that you have accumulated over the years and ensure that your children or other heirs will benefit from it.

In that case, your TFSA should be as risk-free as possible. An easy way to achieve that is to open a GIC plan and invest all the money in guaranteed investment certificates. GICs are covered by deposit insurance up to $100,000 (or more in some cases). Just be sure the issuing institution is a member of the Canada Deposit Insurance Corporation (CDIC) or is covered by a provincial insurance plan.

A laddered GIC portfolio is the best choice. This involves investing 20 percent of the money in GICs that mature in each of the next five years. This ensures that a portion of the cash is available each year, which may be important for estate settlement purposes after your death. If cash is not needed at the time a GIC matures, the proceeds can be rolled over in a new five-year certificate so as to maximize the interest earned.

Most GICs have a minimum investment requirement of $1000, so the laddered approach will work as long as your TFSA has at least $5000 in it.

Action Summary

1. Decide on your priorities before opening a TFSA. The type of plan you choose and the securities you select will be determined in large part by your goals.
2. If you are saving to buy a home, a time frame of no more than five years is recommended. You need to give careful thought to how much risk you will accept.

3. You don't have to invest in penny mining stocks to maximize capital gains. Blue-chip stocks purchased when they're cheap can be surprisingly lucrative.
4. If you use a TFSA for retirement savings, treat it as a personal pension plan.
5. An RESP is the best way to save for a child's education. If you use a TFSA as well, make sure all the assets are in cash or fixed-income securities when the student is ready for college.
6. Older people may wish to use a TFSA to protect their assets for their heirs. GICs are well suited to this purpose.

14

Choosing Your Plan

There are essentially five types of TFSAs: savings accounts, GIC plans, mutual fund plans, multiple-option plans, and self-directed plans. The terms and conditions for each plan may vary considerably, even within the same company, and you may be able to select several types of investment options within a single plan. For example, Bank of Montreal offers five different TFSA options based on guaranteed investment certificates, so customers must be careful to choose the one that best meets their needs.

This chapter contains details about the options offered by a number of financial institutions, including banks, credit unions, insurance companies, and brokerage firms. It does not cover every financial institution in Canada, but the information provided here should help you to assess the competitiveness of plans offered by other companies.

In gathering material for this chapter, our researchers noted that many websites offered few precise details on the terms and conditions of their plans. Generalities abounded, but trying to find out exactly what fees applied or the conditions governing withdrawals could be difficult. Many websites were badly organized, making it difficult even for professional researchers to locate material. For ordinary investors, it would be a nightmare. Perhaps this is being done deliberately in an attempt to force people to contact a representative. But more likely, it's a case of poor design and/or lack of attention.

We also encountered a few organizations that were suspicious of our motives (perhaps they thought we were spying for their competition) and refused to provide information. In those cases, we used whatever was available publicly or simply deleted them from the inclusion list.

Some of the fees we discovered may catch investors by surprise, such as a charge to transfer an account to another institution, which was standard in most cases.

Investors should also be alert to the fact that most financial institutions will automatically roll over GICs for another term unless otherwise instructed.

The information in this chapter was obtained from the listed companies and/or their websites and was believed to be accurate at the time of writing. However, terms and conditions may have changed since (they are constantly evolving). Readers are advised to check with the financial institution of their choice for the most recent details and rates before making any commitments.

Again, please remember that this is not a comprehensive list of every TFSA available in Canada. If the financial institution you deal with is not listed here, check with it for details on the options it offers.

Banks (Schedule I)

BANK OF MONTREAL (BMO)
Area of operation: National
Website: www.bmo.com

Contact phone numbers:
  English: 1-877-225-5266
  French: 1-877-225-5266
  Cantonese and Mandarin: 1-800-665-8800
  Outside Canada and the Continental U.S.: 416-286-9992
  TTY Service for Hearing Impaired Customers:
    1-866-889-0889
Options available: Eight

Options Offered
Option: BMO Tax-Free Savings Account
Type: Savings account
Minimum investment: $50
Access: Contributions and withdrawals can be made at any time.
Fees: None.
Additional information: Interest is paid at current rates and subject to change.

Option: BMO Cashable RateRiser GIC
Type: Cashable guaranteed investment certificate
Minimum investment: $1000
Access: Cashable in full on the 15th day of each month during the first year and on the first and second anniversary of the issue date. No partial redemptions are permitted.
Fees: None.
Additional information: Interest is paid annually to a TFSA Savings Account or compounded annually and paid at maturity. Three-year terms are available. One-year GICs are reinvested at the current rate unless other instructions are provided.

Option: BMO Redeemable Short-Term Investment Certificate
Type: Cashable guaranteed investment certificate
Minimum investment: $1000
Access: This is fully or partially redeemable at any time. No interest is paid if redeemed within 30 days of the issue date. Minimum withdrawal of $1000 while maintaining at least the minimum investment balance is required. Interest is paid up to redemption date or at maturity.
Fees: None.
Additional information: Terms are for 364 days.

Option: BMO RateRiser Plus GIC
Type: Locked-in guaranteed investment certificate
Minimum investment: $1000 or $5000 if monthly interest payment option is chosen.
Access: Not cashable prior to maturity.
Fees: None.
Additional information: The terms are for one to 10 years. The interest is paid annually or is compounded annually and paid at maturity. There is an automatic reinvestment at maturity into a new GIC with the same term length at the interest rate applicable at time of reinvestment, unless other instructions are provided.

Option: BMO Short-Term Investment Certificate
Type: Locked-in guaranteed investment certificate
Minimum investment: $1000
Access: Not cashable prior to maturity. Interest is paid at maturity.
Fees: None.
Additional information: Terms are for 30 to 359 days. There is automatic reinvestment for the same term length at the current rate unless other instructions are provided.

Option: BMO Guaranteed Investment Certificate (GIC)
Type: Locked-in guaranteed investment certificates
Minimum investment: $1000 or $5000 if the monthly interest payment option is chosen.
Access: Not cashable prior to maturity.
Fees: None.
Additional information: There are terms of one to 10 years. Interest is paid annually or is compounded annually and paid at maturity. There is automatic reinvestment at maturity into a new GIC of the same terms at the interest rate applicable at time of reinvestment, unless other instructions are provided.

Option: BMO RateRiser Max (GIC)
Type: Locked-in guaranteed investment certificates
Minimum investment: $1000
Access: Not cashable prior to maturity.
Fees: None.
Additional information: Interest rate increases each year during terms of three or five years. Interest is paid annually or compounded annually and paid at maturity. There is automatic reinvestment at maturity into a new GIC of the same terms at the interest rate applicable at time of reinvestment, unless other instructions are provided.

Option: BMO Mutual Funds
Type: Mutual funds
Minimum investment: Minimum investments are dependent on the fund being purchased.
Access: Any time.
Fees: There are no administration or withdrawal fees for a TFSA. Any applicable fees for the underlying investments will apply.

Additional information: BMO Mutual Funds can be purchased at any of the BMO Bank of Montreal branches but are technically bought from the legal entity of BMO Investments Inc. BMO Mutual Funds can be held in a TFSA provided that it is an investment account. (TFSA accounts are available in branches within which mutual funds cannot be held.)

BANK OF NOVA SCOTIA (SCOTIABANK)
Area of operation: National
Website: www.scotiabank.com
Contact phone number: 1-800-268-9269
Options available: Multiple

Options Offered
Option: Scotia Tax-Free Savings Account
Type: Multiple option plan.
Minimum investment: Depends on the type of securities held. GIC minimums are from $1000 while mutual fund minimums are from $150 to $150,000.
Access: Any time, depending on the type of investment. GICs are restricted by their terms of maturity.
Fees: None.
Additional information: You are allowed to invest in savings accounts, GICs, or mutual funds. Check out the website for a full list of GIC offerings, which includes a list of redeemable/non-redeemable options. Note that Market Powered and Dividend Fund GICs cannot be purchased under this plan. Most GICs have a $1000 minimum investment except for The Ultimate Laddered GIC, which requires a $5000 minimum investment. If interest is paid monthly, the minimum investment is $5000. To invest in

stocks, consider the self-directed plan offered by Scotia McLeod Direct Investing (see separate listing under Brokers).

CANADIAN IMPERIAL BANK OF COMMERCE (CIBC)
Area of operation: National
Website: www.cibc.com
Contact phone numbers:
  TFSA: 1-866-525-8622
  English: 1-800-465-2422
  French: 1-888-337-2422
Options available: Six

Options Offered
Option: CIBC TFSA Tax Advantage Savings Account
Type: Savings account
Minimum investment: $25
Access: Any time.
Fees: None, except for a $100 fee for transferring to another financial institution.
Additional information: There is a "competitive" interest rate on the full balance. Interest is calculated on the full daily closing balance and is paid monthly. Rates are subject to frequent changes.

Option: CIBC Flexible TFSA GIC
Type: Cashable guaranteed investment certificate
Minimum investment: $500
Access: Full or partial redemption is allowed, subject to a minimum withdrawal of $500. At least $500 in principal must remain on deposit after a partial withdrawal; otherwise the full balance of the GIC will be redeemed. Redemptions are not allowed until at least 30 days after the issue date.

Fees: None, except for a $100 fee for transferring to another financial institution.

Additional information: Interest is earned at the guaranteed rate and at maturity. In the event of early withdrawal, full interest to the date of redemption is paid after only 30 days. If you withdraw funds within the first 29 days, no interest is paid.

Option: CIBC TFSA GIC (Redeemable)
Type: Cashable guaranteed investment certificate
Minimum investment: $500
Access to funds: You can withdraw some or all of the funds on any business day prior to maturity at specified early redemption rates.
Fees: None, except a $100 fee for transfer to another financial institution.
Additional information: Terms are available for nine to 36 months. For terms of one year and less, simple interest is paid at maturity. For terms over one year, interest is compounded annually and paid at maturity. This plan guarantees principal and interest, while giving you the option to cash out at any time. Money is deposited for a period of nine months to three years at a guaranteed interest rate. There is the option available to change to other types of CIBC investments without penalty.

Option: CIBC Cashable Escalating Rate TFSA GIC
Type: Cashable guaranteed investment certificate
Minimum investment: $500
Access to funds: You can withdraw all or some of your money (a minimum of $500) on each anniversary date—or up to seven days after that date—and still earn interest. However at least $500 in principal must remain on deposit after a partial withdrawal; otherwise, the full balance of the GIC will be redeemed. If you redeem

within seven days after an anniversary date, you get interest to the redemption date based on the preceding years' interest rate(s) disclosed at the time of purchase. Other than during the annual redemption period referred to above, if a GIC is redeemed before maturity to transfer funds to a TFSA at another financial institution, no interest will be paid and a transfer fee will apply.

Fees: None, except for a $100 fee for transfer to another financial institution.

Additional information: Terms are for three and five years. The rate increases each year of the term. Interest is compounded annually and is paid at maturity. Original investment amount is always guaranteed in full even if you withdraw prior to maturity.

Option: CIBC Escalating Rate TFSA GIC
Type: Locked-in guaranteed investment certificates
Minimum investment: $500
Access to funds: Non-redeemable prior to maturity for any reason other than transferring to a TFSA at another financial institution or to withdraw an excess contribution. If a GIC is redeemed before maturity to transfer funds to a TFSA at another financial institution, no interest will be paid and a transfer fee will apply.

Fees: None, except for a $100 fee to transfer to another financial institution.

Additional information: The principal and interest are automatically rolled over into a CIBC Escalating Rate TFSA GIC for the same term unless you instruct otherwise prior to maturity. The terms available are three and five years. The rate increases each year of the term. Interest is compounded annually and paid at maturity.

Option: CIBC Bonus Rate TFSA GIC
Type: Locked-in guaranteed investment certificate

Minimum investment: $500

Access to funds: Non-redeemable prior to maturity. If a GIC is redeemed before maturity to transfer funds to a TFSA at another financial institution, no interest will be paid and a transfer fee will apply.

Fees: None, except a transfer fee of $100.

Additional information: The terms available include selected short and/or long terms offered on a time-limited basis. For terms of one year and less, simple interest is paid at maturity. For terms of over one year, interest is compounded annually and paid at maturity.

CANADIAN WESTERN BANK

Area of operation: Primarily operates in four western provinces: British Columbia, Alberta, Saskatchewan, and Manitoba

Website: www.cwbank.com

Contact phone number: 1-780-423-8888

Options available: Three

Options Offered

Option: WestEarner Tax-Free Savings Account

Type: Savings account

Minimum investment: None.

Access: Contributions and withdrawals can be made at any time, at your convenience.

Fees: None.

Additional information: Offers interest calculated on daily closing balance and paid on a monthly basis.

Option: WestEarner TFSA GIC

Type: Cashable guaranteed investment certificates

Minimum investment: $1000

Access: Withdrawals can be made at any time.
Fees: None.
Additional information: Available in one- to five-year terms. Your funds can be automatically renewed or transferred to another TFSA at maturity.

Option: WestEarner High Rise TFSA GIC
Type: Locked-in guaranteed investment certificates
Minimum investment: $1000
Access: If you redeem or transfer your investment on your GIC anniversary date, you receive the interest earned up to the anniversary date.
Fees: There is a $25 self-directed administration fee that may be waived (check with the bank). Withdrawal or transfer in full is $50 and partial is $15.
Additional information: There are terms of three to five years. Interest rate escalates over terms and is paid out each anniversary date. If you redeem or transfer investment other than anniversary date and prior to maturity, some restrictions will apply. Self-directed and mutual fund plans are offered through this account as well as Canadian Western Trust (CWT).

CS ALTERNA BANK
Area of operation: National
Website: www.alterna.ca
Contact phone number: 1-877-560-0100
Options available: One

Option: Tax-Free Fixed Term Deposits
Type: Term deposit
Minimum investment: None.

Access: The funds are accessible within two days for non-standard withdrawals.

Fees: None.

Additional information: There are terms available of one, three, or five years. Withdrawal is permitted from TFSA, within the investment terms.

DUNDEE BANK OF CANADA

Area of operation: National

Website: www.dbc.ca

Contact phone number: 1-877-321-3111

Options available: Three

Options Offered

Option: Dundee C$ Investment Savings Account

Type: Savings account

Minimum investment: None.

Access: Redeemable after a 10-day hold.

Fees: None.

Additional information: Ask about transfer fees or closing charges.

Option: Dundee C$ Investment Short-Term GICs

Type: Cashable guaranteed investment certificate

Minimum investment: $5000

Access: Redeemable after 30 days. Interest is paid up to the day you cash out.

Fees: None.

Additional information: Terms are offered as follows: 30–59 days, 60–89 days, 90–179 days, and 180–364 days. Interest rates may vary depending on the term selected.

Option: Dundee C$ Investment Long-Term GIC
Type: Locked-in guaranteed investment certificate
Minimum investment: $1000
Access: No access to the funds until the GIC matures.
Fees: None.
Additional information: Interest rate will be higher than for cashable GICs but your money will be locked in.

LAURENTIAN BANK OF CANADA
Area of operation: National
Website: www.laurentianbank.ca
Contact phone number: 1-877-522-3863
TTY (text telephone for hearing-impaired customers):
    1-866-262-2231
Options available: One

Option: Tactical TFSA
Type: Multiple option
Minimum investment: $500
Access: Term deposits and mutual funds are redeemable at any time, while GICs cannot be redeemed until maturity.
Fees: None, except for a transfer fee of $65 that may be applied in whole or in part.
Additional information: You can choose from cash accounts, guaranteed investment certificates (GICs), redeemable term deposits, mutual funds, and bonds. All investments are listed on the same statement. You can choose from different GIC families: Multi-Rater is a progressive-rate GIC that is redeemable or reinvestable each year, depending on the product. Action GICs are indexed products, and Xtra GIC has a reinvestment option.

MANULIFE BANK
Area of operation: National
Website: www1.manulifebank.ca
Contact phone number: 1-877-765-2265
Options available: Two

Options Offered
Option: Tax-Free Advantage Account
Type: Savings account
Minimum investment: None.
Access: Arranged through your financial adviser.
Fees: None.
Additional information: Manulife Bank's website offers no information about their TFSAs. Contact a representative or your financial adviser for more details.

Option: Tax-Free Guaranteed Investment Certificates
Type: Locked-in guaranteed investment certificate
Minimum investment: $2500
Access: Only at maturity.
Fees: None.
Additional information: Terms are available for one to five years.

NATIONAL BANK
Area of operation: National
Website: www.nbc.ca
Contact phone number: 1-877-394-6611
ATS (hearing impaired): 1-866-494-6742
Options available: Seven

Options Offered
Option: Tax-Free Savings Accounts—Cash Balance
Type: Savings account
Minimum investment: $25
Access: The money is available at all times.
Fees: None.
Additional information: Contact the branch adviser or the customer service (Telnat) for withdrawals. Money can be transferred via bank account with National Bank or by cheque.

Option: Tax-Free Guaranteed Investment Certificates (Redeemable)
Type: Cashable guaranteed investment certificate
Minimum investment: $500
Access: Any time. However, if redeemed within 30 days of the issue date, no interest is paid.
Fees: None, except for a $50 transfer fee to another financial institution.
Additional information: Terms are one to five years. The interest rate is fixed for the entire term. You can purchase without an account with bank, except for website contributions.

Option: Tax-Free Guaranteed Investment Certificates (Non-redeemable)
Type: Locked-in guaranteed investment certificate
Minimum investment: $500
Access: Non-redeemable prior to maturity.
Fees: None, except for a $50 transfer fee to another financial institution.
Additional information: Terms available: one to five years.

Option: Tax-Free Guaranteed Investment Certificates (Non-redeemable with unconventional term)
Type: Locked-in guaranteed investment certificate
Minimum investment: $1000
Access: Non-redeemable prior to maturity.
Fees: None, except for a $50 transfer fee to another financial institution.
Additional information: The interest rate is fixed for the entire term. Interest paid annually or at maturity date. Non-transferable. Terms available: 14 to 51 months.

Option: Tax-Free Guaranteed Investment Certificates (Non-redeemable Escalator)
Type: Locked-in guaranteed investment certificate
Minimum investment: $500
Access: Non-redeemable prior to maturity.
Fees: None, except for a $50 transfer fee to another financial institution.
Additional information: Terms available are for one to five years. The rates are determined at issuance. Interest rate increases each year.

Option: Tax-Free Guaranteed Investment Variable-Yield GICs
Type: Market-rate guaranteed investment certificate
Minimum investment: $500
Access: Non-redeemable prior to maturity.
Fees: None, except for a $50 transfer fee to another financial institution.
Additional information: Terms available: one to five years. Rate increases each year. Internet contributions not permitted.

Option: Mutual Fund TFSA
Type: Mutual funds
Minimum investment: $500
Access: Client access to money via brokerage platform.
Fees: No specific fees quoted—inquire.
Additional information: National Bank Securities, Altamira, and Omega mutual funds. Periodic investments are offered at a minimum of $25 with National Bank mutual funds. Other fund families are also available with their minimum investment normally $50 or $100.

PRESIDENT'S CHOICE FINANCIAL
Area of operation: National
Website: www.banking.pcfinancial.ca
Contact phone number: 1-866-884-3434
Options available: One

Option: Tax-Free Interest Plus Savings Account
Type: Savings account
Minimum investment: No minimum deposit to open account.
Access: Any time.
Fees: None.
Additional information: Bonus interest paid when balance exceeds $1000. You can access funds via telephone and online banking, or at any CIBC or President's Choice ABM.

ROYAL BANK
Area of operation: National
Website: www.royalbank.com
Contact phone number: 1-800-463-3863
Number of TFSA products: One

Option: RBC Tax-Free Savings Account
Type: Multiple option
Minimum investment: $100 ($25 for an automatic contribution plan).
Access: Any time, subject to any restrictions on investments in plan (for example, locked-in GICs).
Fees: None, other than MERs on mutual funds.
Additional information: Offers choice of savings account, GICs, and RBC mutual funds.

TD CANADA TRUST
Area of operation: National
Website: www.tdcanadatrust.com
Contact phone numbers:
 English: 1-866-222-3456
 French: 1-800-895-4463
 Cantonese/Mandarin: 1-800-387-2828
 TTY (text telephone): 1-800-361-1180
Options available: Six

Options Offered
Option: Tax-Free Savings Account
Type: Savings account
Minimum investment: None.
Access: Any time.
Fees: No administration fees.
Additional information: It is possible to maintain a high-interest TFSA or purchase GICs and term deposits through this account.

Option: High Interest TFSA Savings Account
Type: Savings account

Minimum investment: None.

Access: Any time.

Fees: No administration fees. There is one free debit per month and each additional debit is $5.

Additional information: Your money is transferable at any time. The account is accessible online, by phone, at the branch, and through ATM.

Option: Term Deposit TFSA

Type: Term deposit

Minimum investment: $1000 for long term, $5000 for short term.

Access: Can be redeemed early—contact a representative.

Fees: None.

Additional information: Long-term deposits from one to five years.

Option: GIC TFSA

Type: Guaranteed investment certificate

Minimum investment: $1000 for long term; $5000 for short term

Access: GICs are normally locked in until maturity.

Fees: None.

Additional information: GICs can be accessed online and over the phone. Contact a representative to make changes; for example, early redemption.

Option: Market Growth GIC TFSA

Type: Index-linked guaranteed investment certificate

Minimum investment: $1000

Access: Not redeemable prior to maturity

Fees: None.

Additional information: Principal will be repaid at maturity. Changes in the index to which the return on a Market Growth GIC is linked will affect the interest payable on the GIC. The five types of Market Growth GICs are GIC Plus, US GIC Plus, Global GIC Plus, Financials GIC Plus, and Utilities GIC Plus. The Security GIC Plus is not considered a Market Growth GIC, as it has a guaranteed minimum return.

Option: TD Mutual Funds Tax-Free Savings Account
Type: Mutual funds
Minimum investment: TD Mutual Funds have minimum initial and subsequent investment thresholds.
Access: Any time.
Fees: Most TD Mutual Funds charge an early redemption fee within a certain number of days after purchase.
Additional information: Variety of asset categories, currencies, sectors, geographic regions, and management styles. TD Comfort Portfolios are offered. Mutual fund representatives with TD Investment Services Inc. distribute mutual funds at TD Canada Trust.

Banks (Schedule II)

CITIBANK CANADA
Area of operation: National
Website: www.citi.com/canada/homepage/english/index.jsp
Contact phone number: 1-800-387-1616
Options available: Three

Options Offered
Option: Citibank High Interest TFSA
Type: Savings account
Minimum investment: None.
Access: Any time.
Fees: None.
Additional information: Free access to your account any time via Citibank Online and the CitiPhone Banking Centre.

Option: Citibank GIC TFSA—(Cashable)
Type: Cashable guaranteed investment certificate
Minimum investment: $1000
Access: Redeemable at any time before maturity.
Fees: None.
Additional information: Option of interest paid annually or compounded annually and paid at maturity.

Option: Citibank GIC TFSA—Non-Redeemable
Type: Locked-in guaranteed investment certificate
Minimum investment: $1000
Access: Redeemable only at maturity.
Fees: None.
Additional information: Option of interest paid annually or compounded annually and paid at maturity.

HSBC BANK CANADA
Area of operation: National
Website: www.hsbc.ca
Contact phone number: 1-888-310-4722
Options available: Four

Options Offered

Option: Direct Tax-Free Savings Account

Type: Savings account

Minimum investment: None.

Access: Any time.

Fees: Transfer fee of $25 to another financial institution. ATM fees may apply.

Additional information: Online, telephone, and ATM access only. No-fee withdrawals through HSBC ATMs or in bank. Fee applies to withdrawals through other ATMs. No interest will be paid unless you have at least $1000 in the account.

Option: TFSA High Rate Savings Account

Type: Savings account

Minimum investment: None.

Access: Any time.

Fees: $5 fee for self-serve debit transaction and a $5 fee for in-bank withdrawal. Transfer fee of $25 to another financial institution.

Additional information: Pays same rate as Direct Account unless your balance is very high. Check website or branch for more details.

Option: TFSA Redeemable GIC

Type: Cashable guaranteed investment certificate

Minimum investment: $1000

Access: Redeem prior to maturity with no interest penalty after 89 days.

Fees: Early redemption rates apply.

Additional information: Invest funds at a fixed rate for a one-year term with the ability to redeem prior to maturity with no interest penalty after 89 days. Interest paid at time of redemption or at maturity. Select term deposits and GICs booked through HSBC's internet banking may be eligible for special pricing. Log on to Internet Banking for more details.

Option: TFSA Term Deposit
Type: Cashable term deposit
Minimum investment: $1000
Access: Redeemable prior to maturity, though you receive no interest.
Fees: Early redemption rates apply.
Additional information: $1000 minimum deposit for annual or semi-annual interest payment options; $5000 minimum deposit for monthly or at maturity interest payment options. Automatic renewal of investments unless advised prior to maturity (option to renew principal only or principal plus interest). Terms of 30 days to five years. Interest is not compounded and is paid at the intervals shown. Special pricing may be offered through internet banking.

ING DIRECT
Area of operation: National
Website: www.ingdirect.ca/en
Contact phone number: 1-877-700-1737
Options available: Four

Options Offered
Option: ING DIRECT Tax-Free Investment Savings Account
Type: Savings account
Minimum investment: None.
Access: Any time.
Fees: None.

Additional information: Interest may be higher than at major banks. Compare rates.

Option: Tax-Free Guaranteed Investment (GIC)
Type: Cashable guaranteed investment certificate
Minimum investment: None.
Access: Any time after maturity.
Fees: None.
Additional information: Cashable rate option.

Option: Tax-Free Short Term Guaranteed Investment (GIC)
Type: Locked-in guaranteed investment certificate
Minimum investment: None.
Access: You can cash out early if you waive the interest you might otherwise receive.
Fees: None.
Additional information: Terms: 90, 180, or 270 days. Interest is calculated daily and paid at maturity. You can roll over into the same term again or transfer to a savings account.

Option: Mutual Funds Account (Streetwise Fund)
Minimum investment: None.
Access: Any time.
Fees: 1-percent MER.
Additional information: No commissions payable. Selection is limited: a balanced fund, balanced income fund, and balanced growth fund.

ICICI BANK CANADA
Area of operation: Alberta, British Columbia, and Ontario
Website: www.icicbank.ca

Contact phone number: 1-888-424-2422
Options available: Two

Options Offered
Option: Tax-Free Savings Account (TFSA)
Type: Savings account
Minimum investment: None.
Access: Instant withdrawal from account.
Fees: A charge of $25 for transfers to another financial institution. For account closure between 14 days to six months of opening date, a fee of $25 will apply.
Additional information: Interest credited monthly.

Option: Tax-Free GIC
Type: Cashable guaranteed investment certificate
Minimum investment: $1000
Access: Early redemptions are possible.
Fees: A charge of $25 for transfers to another financial institution. For account closure between 14 days to six months of opening date, a fee of $25 will apply.
Additional information: Terms from one to five years. Interest credited monthly.

Brokers

BMO INVESTORLINE
Area of operation: National
Website: www.bmoinvestorline.com
Contact phone number: 1-888-776-6886
Options available: One

Option: BMO InvestorLine TFSA
Type: Self-directed
Minimum investment: $1000
Access: Full or partial withdrawals at any time.
Fees: Annual administration fee of $50 unless total assets exceed $100,000. Transfer out: $135 for full account; $50 for partial account. Swaps: $45.
Additional information: Discount brokerage account. Taxes may apply on fees. Other fees may apply such as commissions, security registration, and estate account certificate. A charge of $20 may be levied on account balances of less than $5000 (may be waived if at least two commissionable trades are completed). More details at bmoinvestorline.com.

BMO NESBITT BURNS
Area of operation: National
Website: www.bmonesbittburns.com
Contact phone number: 1-416-359-4000
Options available: One

Option: BMO Nesbitt Burns TFSA
Type: Self-directed
Minimum investment: Not available.
Access: Consult investment adviser.
Fees: Annual administration fee: $50. Transfer out: full or partial account $135. Withdrawal: full or partial $15/request.
Additional information: Full-service brokerage account. Get details from a representative. No mention of TFSAs on website as of time of writing.

CIBC INVESTOR'S EDGE
Area of operation: National
Website: www.investorsedge.cibc.com/ie/tfsa/index.html
Contact phone number: 1-800-567-3343
Options available: One

Option: CIBC Investor's Edge TFSA
Type: Self-directed
Minimum investment: Not available.
Access: Consult investment adviser.
Fees: Brokerage commissions charged. Inquire about other fees.
Additional information: Discount brokerage account.

DESJARDINS SECURITIES
Area of operation: National
Website: www1.vmd.ca
Contact phone number: 1-888-987-1749
Options available: One

Option: Desjardins Securities TFSA
Type: Self-directed
Minimum investment: Check with an adviser.
Access: Any time, unless there are product restrictions.
Fees: Closing fees: $135 plus taxes. Transfer of securities to a TFSA: $25. Partial transfer outside Desjardins Group: $125 plus taxes. Transfer outside Desjardins Group: $25 per security.
Additional information: Full-service brokerage plan for all market-traded products, GICs, and cash account.

DISNAT ONLINE BROKERAGE
Area of operation: National
Website: www.disnat.com
Contact phone number: 1-866-873-7103
Options available: One

Option: Disnat Online Brokerage TFSA
Type: Self-directed
Minimum investment: $1000 or minimum regular instalments of $25.
Access: Any time.
Fees: None, except transfer of securities to a TFSA: $25. Partial transfer outside Desjardins Group: $125 plus taxes. Transfer outside Desjardins Group: $25 per security.
Additional information: Discount brokerage account. All market-traded products available.

HSBC INVESTDIRECT
Area of operation: National
Website: http://investdirect.hsbc.ca
Contact phone number: 1-800-830-8888
Options available: One

Option: HSBC Invest Direct Tax Free Savings Account (TFSA)
Type: Self-directed
Minimum investment: Depends on products used. GIC minimums are $1000 to $5000. Mutual funds: $1000 (initial purchase); $500 for any purchase thereafter.
Access: Any time but restrictions may apply depending on type of security.
Fees: Trading commissions may apply.

Additional information: Can invest in GICs, stocks, bonds, and more than 1200 mutual funds.

NATIONAL BANK FINANCIAL
Area of operation: National
Website: www.nbdb.ca
Contact phone number: 1-800-363-3511
Options available: One

Option: National Bank Financial TFSA
Type: Self-directed.
Minimum investment: $1000
Access: Any time.
Fees: $50 annual administration fee, waived when the plan holds National Bank Financial Group products. Partial or complete transfer-out fees: $135.
Additional information: Full-service brokerage, can be used to park cash or to purchase stocks. Minimum investment depends on the characteristics of the product bought by the client. Five free substitutions per year.

NATIONAL BANK DIRECT BROKERAGE
Area of operation: National
Website: www.nbdb.ca
Contact phone number: 1-800-363-3511
Options available: One

Option: National Bank Direct Brokerage TFSA
Type: Self-directed
Minimum investment: $1000 (cash balance)
Access: Any time, providing there are no product restrictions.

Fees: Annual administration fees of $50 will apply in certain situations. Partial or complete transfer-out fees: $135.

Additional information: Discount brokerage account. May be used for cash or for securities purchases. Annual fees may be waived if one of these options applies: 100 percent National Bank Financial Group products; total worth in the account (non-registered and TFSA) is over $100,000; minimum of two transactions generating commissions have been done in the previous 12 months, ending May 31.

QTRADE INVESTOR ONLINE BROKERAGE
Area of operation: National
Website: www.qtrade.ca
Contact phone number: 1-877-787-2330
Options available: One

Option: Tax-Free Savings Account
Type: Self-directed
Minimum investment: $1000 ($2000 for margin accounts).
Access: Can make partial withdrawals at no charge. However, you have to complete an RSP/RIF/TFSA Deregistration form.
Fees: No administration fees. Normal trading commission apply. Account closing fee: $75. Supplemental fee for accounts closed within one year: $50. (Both of these fees would be charged if you withdraw all the funds and close the account within one year of opening.)
Additional information: Discount brokerage account.

QUESTRADE INVESTOR
Area of operation: National
Website: www.questrade.com

Contact phone number: 1-888-783-7866
Options available: Two

Options Offered
Option: The Questrade Tax-Free Trading Account
Type: Self-directed trading/investing account
Minimum investment: $1000
Access: Any time.
Fees: No fees to open or close account, and no inactive fee. Specific fees such as commissions for mutual funds and securities trading will apply.
Additional information: Direct trading account. Trades in all major North American markets. Clients can settle trades in U.S. or Canadian currency. Also offers gold bullion trading.

Option: Mutual Fund Maximizer
Type: Mutual funds
Minimum investment: $1000
Access: Any time.
Fees: Commission of $9.95 per trade.
Additional information: Offers the option of putting mutual fund trailer fee rebates back to client's TFSA. These are not considered as contributions, so do not affect contribution room.

RBC DIRECT INVESTING
Area of operation: National
Website: www.rbcdirectinvesting.com
Contact phone numbers:
   General and Trading Inquiries: 1-800-769-2560
   General and Trading Inquiries in Cantonese/Mandarin:
      1-800-667-8668
Options available: One

Option: RBC Direct Investing Tax-Free Savings Account
Type: Self-directed
Minimum investment: None.
Access: Can withdraw money at any time, providing the investment is in a liquid format. For example, stocks and bonds must be converted to cash. Investments in non-redeemable GICs cannot be cashed prior to maturity.
Fees: No fees but trading commissions apply.
Additional information: Discount brokerage account. Offers ability to open account online if you have an account with them. Trading commissions start from $6.95 to $9.95. Can purchase stocks, bonds, fixed-income securities, and more than 2500 mutual funds as part of portfolios.

RBC DOMINION SECURITIES

Area of operation: National
Website: www.rbcds.com
Contact phone number: 1-800-561-6431
Options available: One

Option: RBC DS Tax-Free Savings Account
Type: Self-directed
Minimum investment: None specified.
Access: Two free withdrawals a year. Cash withdrawals can be made immediately. Withdrawals requiring the sales of securities may take up to three business days.
Fees: There is an annual investment management fee of 1 percent of the plan's net asset value as of October 31. Accounts that are closed prior to October month-end will be charged the 1-percent fee prior to the account being closed, based on the previous month-end market value. Substitution fee: $25 (first two free each

year). Withdrawal fee: $25 (first two free each year). Deregistration fee $100.

Additional information: Full-service brokerage firm. Eight free trades a year. F-class mutual funds are used.

SCOTIA ITRADE
Area of operation: National
Website: www.scotiaitrade.com
Contact phone number: 1-888-872-3388
Options available: One

Option: Scotia iTrade Tax-Free Savings Account
Type: Self-directed
Minimum investment: Only specific products require minimum investments: GICs: $1000 to $5000; mutual funds: varies depending on fund; stocks: depends on market price.
Access: Funds can be accessed any time.
Fees: No annual administration fees. Trades cost $6.99.
Additional information: Discount brokerage account. Choose from more than 3200 mutual funds, stocks, ETFs, and fixed-income securities.

SCOTIA McLEOD DIRECT INVESTING
Area of operation: National
Website: www.scotiabank.com/cda/content/0,,CID598_LIDen,00.html
Contact phone number: 1-800-263-3430
Options available: One

Option: Self-Directed Tax Free Savings Account
Type: Self-directed

Minimum investment: Only specific products require minimum investments: GICs: $1000 to $5000; mutual funds: varies depending on fund; stocks: depends on market price.

Access: Any time, depending on product.

Fees: Annual administration fees, partial withdrawal fees, and deregistration of plan fees do not apply to Tax-Free Savings Accounts. Brokerage commissions applicable. Swaps: fee of $35 per security may apply. Transfers (full/partial): $125 per transfer may apply. More information about fees can be obtained at www.scotiabank.com/cda/content/0,1608,CID5660_LIDen,00. html#Self_Directed.

Additional information: Discount brokerage account. There are more than 2500 mutual funds to choose from as well as all other qualified securities that are publicly traded.

TD WATERHOUSE

Area of operation: National

Website: www.tdwaterhouse.ca

Contact phone number: 1-800-465-5463

Options available: One

Option: TD Waterhouse Tax-Free Savings Account

Type: Self-directed

Minimum investment: Generally none, but it depends on type of investment.

Access: Any time.

Fees: Administration fee: $50. First withdrawal per year is free. Further withdrawals in the same year: $25. Termination or full transfer fee: $125. Partial transfer: $25 per asset, to a maximum of $125. Swaps: $45. Fees subject to change.

Additional information: Administration fee is waived when household assets are $100,000 or over. Administration fee is also waived when the client registers for eServices (online statements, confirmations, and tax receipts). Can contribute, withdraw, or swap assets in-kind or in-cash. Qualified investments include domestic and foreign equities, GICs, bonds, publicly traded shares, and mutual funds. Also available: Managed Solutions (TD MAP) and fixed income (bonds, GICs, mortgage-backed securities).

TRADEFREEDOM
Area of operation: National
Website: www.tradefreedom.com
Contact phone number: 1-800-706-7835
Options available: One

Option: TradeFreedom TFSA
Type: Self-directed
Minimum investment: None specified.
Access: Any time.
Fees: Trades from $6.99.
Additional information: Discount brokerage account. Full range of qualified securities and mutual funds available.

Credit Unions

ALTERNA SAVINGS
Area of operation: Ontario
Website: www.alterna.ca
Contact phone number: 1-877-560-0100
Options available: Four

Options Offered

Option: High Interest Investment Savings Account

Type: Savings account

Minimum investment: None.

Access: Funds accessible within two days for non-standard withdrawals.

Fees: None.

Additional information: Must be a member of the credit union to open an account (applies to all TFSAs).

Option: One-Year Closed Term Deposit

Type: Locked-in term deposit

Minimum investment: $500

Access: Not redeemable until maturity.

Fees: None.

Option: Three-Year Closed Fixed Term Deposit

Type: Locked-in term deposit

Minimum investment: $500

Access: Complete access available on maturity.

Fees: None.

Option: Five-Year Fixed Term Deposit

Type: Locked-in term deposit

Minimum investment: $500 or $5000 depending on type of investment.

Access: Complete access on maturity

Fees: None.

Additional information: Two tiers available. If you invest $500 to $4999, a lower level of interest rate is offered. Higher rate applies over $5000.

ASSINIBOINE CREDIT UNION
Area of operation: Manitoba
Website: www.assiniboine.mb.ca
Contact phone number: 1-877-958-8588
Options available: Three

Options Offered
Option: ACU's Tax-Free Savings Account
Type: Savings account
Minimum investment: None
Access: Any time.
Fees: $1 for any type of withdrawal.
Additional information: Must be a member of the credit union.

Option: ACU's GICs (Redeemable)
Type: Cashable guaranteed investment certificate
Minimum investment: $1000
Access: Can be accessed in the first 30 days but lose all interest paid. No penalty thereafter.
Fees: $1 for any type of withdrawal.
Additional information: Lower interest rate than for non-redeemable GICs.

Option: ACU's GICs (2–5 years)
Type: Locked-in guaranteed investment certificate
Minimum investment: $1000
Access: Non-redeemable until maturity.
Fees: $1 for any type of withdrawal.
Additional information: Can also buy mutual funds through Credential Asset Management Inc.

COAST CAPITAL SAVINGS
Area of operation: British Columbia
Website: www.coastcapitalsavings.com
Contact phone number: 1-888-517-7000
Options available: Six

Options Offered
Option: Tax-Free Savings Account
Type: Savings account with six escalating interest tiers
Minimum investment: None.
Access: Any time.
Fees: None.
Additional information: The six tiers depend on the amount in the account.

Option: High-interest No-fee Savings Account
Type: High-interest savings account
Minimum investment: None.
Access: Unlimited.
Fees: None.
Additional information: Premium interest rate paid.

Option: Watch-It-Grow
Type: Term deposit
Minimum investment: $20 a week.
Access: Redeemable with full interest after six months.
Fees: None.
Additional information: Automatic contribution plan. Available in six- and 12-month terms.

Option: Rising Rate Tax-Free Savings Account
Type: Locked-in guaranteed investment certificate
Minimum investment: $1000
Access: Money can be taken out with full interest on each anniversary date.
Fees: None.
Additional information: Available in three- or seven-year terms. Interest rate increases annually. On each anniversary date you can increase to a higher rate or withdraw from account.

Option: GIC Tax-Free Savings Account
Type: Locked-in guaranteed investment certificate
Minimum investment: $1000
Access: Principal is locked in until maturity. However, interest can be paid out.
Fees: None.
Additional information: Available in terms from 30 days to five years. Compound interest option available if cash flow not required. Automatically renews for the same term at maturity unless instructions given to the contrary.

Option: Mutual Funds TFSA
Type: Mutual funds
Minimum investment: $50
Access: Not locked in. Buy or sell any time.
Fees: Depends on type of mutual funds.
Additional information: Automatic deposits as low as $50 a month.

DESJARDINS GROUP

Area of operation: National
Website: www.desjardins.com
Contact phone number: 1-888-517-7000
Options available: 17

Options Offered
Option: Savings Accounts—TFSA
Type: Savings account
Minimum investment: None.
Access: Cashable when required.
Fees: None, except for $50 plus taxes when transferred outside Desjardins Group.
Additional information: Minimum automatic regular investment: $25. Frequency of automatic regular investment: weekly, every two weeks, twice monthly.

Option: Term Savings—TFSA
Type: Term deposit
Minimum investment: $500
Access: Redeemable before maturity under certain conditions.
Fees: None, except for $50 plus taxes when transferred outside of Desjardins Group.
Additional information: Interest rate is fixed, guaranteed until maturity. Terms are for 30 days to 10 years.

Option: Regular Deposit Term Savings—TFSA
Type: Term deposit
Minimum investment: $1200 for one-year term; $3000 for other terms (to five years).

Access: Redeemable in full without penalty on the third and fourth anniversary dates of the deposit, under certain conditions.
Fees: None, except $50 plus taxes when transferred outside Desjardins Group.
Additional information: Includes different options for automatic regular investment: weekly, every two weeks, twice monthly, monthly.

Option: Redeemable Term Savings—TFSA
Type: Term deposit
Minimum investment: $1000
Access: Redeemable in full or in part at any time without penalty.
Fees: None, except $50 plus taxes when transferred outside Desjardins Group.
Additional information: Interest rate fixed, guaranteed until maturity. Terms are available for one year.

Option: Redeemable Climbing-Rate Term Savings—TFSA
Type: Term deposit
Minimum investment: $1000
Access: Redeemable on the anniversary date totally or partially without penalty, under certain conditions.
Fees: None, except $50 plus taxes when transferred outside Desjardins Group.
Additional information: Interest rate increases from year to year. Terms are of three or five years.

Option: Climbing-Rates Term Savings—TFSA
Type: Term deposit
Minimum investment: $1000

Access: Non-redeemable before maturity. On the deposit anniversary date, can be converted totally or partially to a non-redeemable term savings plan or a mutual fund available at a Caisse Desjardins.
Fees: None, except $50 plus taxes when transferred outside Desjardins Group.
Additional information: Interest rate: increases from year to year. Terms: Three or five years.

Option: Diversified Term Savings—TFSA
Type: Term deposit
Minimum investment: $3000
Access: Option to withdraw all or part of one of the segments.
Fees: None, except $50 plus taxes when transferred outside Desjardins Group.
Additional information: Interest rate fixed, guaranteed until maturity. Terms from one to three years (for investments divided into three segments); from one to four years (for investments divided into four segments); from one to five years (for investments divided into five segments).

Option: Regular Income Term Savings—TFSA
Type: Term deposit
Minimum investment: $1000
Access: One lump-sum amount per year without charge or penalty, under certain conditions.
Fees: None, except $50 plus taxes when transferred outside Desjardins Group.
Additional information: Interest rate is fixed, guaranteed until maturity. Terms: one year to five years. Frequency of automatic regular investment: weekly, every two weeks, twice monthly, monthly.

Option: Student Savings Account—TFSA
Type: Savings account
Minimum investment: None.
Access: $300 minimum for partial withdrawals with account balance maintained above $500.
Fees: None, except $50 plus taxes when transferred outside Desjardins Group.
Additional information: The goal is to save $500 over 12 months. You can pay through automatic regular investment. Minimum amount depends on frequency of payment. Weekly: $10. Every two weeks: $20. Twice a month: $25. Monthly: $45.

Option: Stock Market-Indexed Guaranteed Investment
Type: Market-linked guaranteed investments
Minimum investment: $500
Access: Not redeemable before maturity.
Fees: None, except $50 plus taxes when transferred outside Desjardins Group.
Additional information: Capital 100 percent guaranteed. Returns based on the increase in value of the stock market index. A rate of participation in index growth or maximum growth may apply. Terms of three and a half to five years.

Option: Natural Resource Guaranteed Investment
Type: Market-linked guaranteed investments
Minimum investment: $500
Access: Not redeemable before maturity.
Fees: None, except $50 plus taxes when transferred outside Desjardins Group.
Additional information: Capital 100 percent guaranteed. Returns based on the price variations of natural resources commodities:

energy, industrial metals, precious metals, and agricultural. Terms of five years.

Option: Global Equity Guaranteed Investment
Type: Market-linked guaranteed investments
Minimum investment: $500
Access: Not redeemable before maturity.
Fees: None, except $50 plus taxes when transferred outside Desjardins Group.
Additional information: Capital 100 percent guaranteed. Returns linked to a portfolio of 15 international large-cap corporations. Terms of three and a half to five years.

Option: Desjardins Enhanced Return Guaranteed Investment
Type: Market-linked guaranteed investments
Minimum investment: $500
Access: Redeemable before maturity under certain conditions
Fees: None, except $50 plus taxes when transferred outside Desjardins Group.
Additional information: Capital 100 percent guaranteed. Returns linked to a portfolio of eight Canadian stocks selected from the largest banking and insurance businesses or linked to a portfolio of 10 stocks selected from major international businesses in the consumer staples and health-care industries. Terms of three and a half to six years.

Option: Desjardins Profile Guaranteed Investment Portfolio
Type: Market-linked guaranteed investments
Minimum investment: $1000
Access: Not redeemable before maturity.

Fees: None, except $50 plus taxes when transferred outside Desjardins Group.

Additional information: Capital 100 percent guaranteed. Returns based on portfolio composition of the following: Term Savings, Desjardins Enhanced Return Guaranteed Investment (Financial Services, Consumer Staples, Health Care), and Desjardins Equity Guaranteed Investment Portfolio. Terms of five years.

Option: Desjardins Equity Guaranteed Investment Portfolio
Type: Market-linked guaranteed investments
Minimum investment: $1000
Access: Not redeemable before maturity.
Fees: None, except $50 plus taxes when transferred outside Desjardins Group.
Additional information: Returns based on the performance of Canadian, American, and overseas indices. Terms of up to five years.

Option: Desjardins Mutual Funds
Type: Mutual funds
Minimum investment: $1000
Access: Consult representative.
Fees: None, except $50 plus taxes when transfer outside Desjardins Group.
Additional information: This includes funds from areas of income, balanced, equity, and special.

Option: Guaranteed Investment Funds—Helios Contract—TFSA
Type: Mutual funds
Minimum investment: $5000
Access: Any time.

Fees: May be incurred related to the investment funds and the guarantees. Otherwise none, including no transfer fees for accounts referred by a Caisse Desjardins to Desjardins Financial Security.

Additional information: The Helios Contract is offered by financial security advisers of Desjardins Financial Security. Offers access to 33 investment funds, including six portfolios. Guarantees protect against market downturns. There is an optional guarantee of predictable income for life.

ENVISION FINANCIAL

Area of operation: British Columbia
Website: www.envisionfinancial.ca
Contact phone number: Call local branch. See website for numbers.
Options available: Nine

Options Offered
Option: High Interest Savings Account
Type: Savings account
Minimum investment: None.
Access: Complete access.
Fees: ATM fees.
Additional information: Can access via ATM. You get one free transaction.

Option: 12-Month Cashable
Type: Cashable term deposit
Minimum investment: $1000
Access: Cashable after 30 days.
Fees: Transfer out and close out fees: $50.
Additional information: If cashed after 30 days, you will receive interest with no penalty.

Option: 18-Month Cashable Term Deposit
Type: Cashable term deposit
Minimum investment: $1000
Access: Cashable after the first six months
Fees: Transfer out and close out fees: $50.
Additional information: If cashed after six months, you receive interest with no penalty.

Option: StepUp 9 Plus 9
Type: Cashable term deposit
Minimum investment: $1000
Access: Fully cashable at any time.
Fees: Transfer out and close out fees: $50.
Additional information: Term is 18 months. Interest is divided into two stages, with an increase halfway through the term. Interest paid annually.

Option: StepUp 18 Plus 18
Type: Cashable term deposit
Minimum investment: $1000
Access: Fully cashable at any time.
Fees: Transfer out and close out fees: $50.
Additional information: Similar to 9 Plus 9 plan but term is longer.

Option: TOP5
Type: Cashable term deposit
Minimum investment: $1000
Access: You can withdraw up to 20 percent of your original deposit without any penalty.
Fees: Transfer out and close out fees: $50.

Additional information: Five-year term deposit. TOP5 pays an annual return based on the interest rate at either the time of deposit (that is, the base rate) or the current posted five-year rate—whichever is higher. Automatic renewal. Interest is paid annually. Rate is reset annually (on the anniversary date) to the current five-year rate and will never go below the "guaranteed rate."

Option: Market-linked enhanced return guaranteed investment
Type: Market-linked GIC
Minimum investment: $1000
Access: Only at maturity.
Fees: Transfer out and close out fees: $50.
Additional information: Three- to five-year terms. Guaranteed principal and minimum return.

Option: Short Term Non-Redeemable
Type: Locked-in term deposit
Minimum investment: $1000
Access: Non-redeemable prior to maturity.
Fees: Transfer out and close out fees: $50.
Additional information: Terms up to 364 days. Interest compounds semi-annually for registered terms over six months (otherwise interest is paid at maturity). Automatic renewal of investment. Deposits are 100 percent guaranteed by the Credit Union Deposit Insurance Corporation of British Columbia.

Option: Long Term Non-Redeemable
Type: Locked-in term deposit
Minimum investment: $1000
Access: Redeemable with a 2-percent penalty.
Fees: Transfer out and close out fees: $50.

Additional information: Available in one- to five-year terms. A good choice if you are looking to maximize your return but want to be able to access your investment.

FIRST CALGARY SAVINGS
Area of operation: Calgary
Website: www.1stcalgary.com
Contact phone number: 1-866-923-4778
Options available: Six

Options Offered
Option: Non-redeemable Term Deposits
Type: Locked-in short-term deposit
Minimum investment: $5000
Access: Non-redeemable before maturity.
Fees: None.
Additional information: Terms from 30 to 364 days.

Option: Non-redeemable Term Deposits
Type: Locked-in long-term deposit
Minimum investment: $500
Access: Non-redeemable before maturity.
Fees: None.
Additional information: Terms from one year to five years.

Option: Step-Up 6PLUS6 Deposits
Type: Cashable term deposit
Minimum investment: $500
Access: Redeemable at any time providing amount is over $500.
Fees: None.

Additional information: Offers different interest rates in two periods. First six months lower; second six months higher. Call for specific rates.

Option: Step-Up 9PLUS9 Deposits
Type: Locked-in term deposit
Minimum investment: $500
Access: Non-redeemable before maturity.
Fees: None.
Additional information: Offers different interest rates in two periods. First nine months lower; second nine months higher.

Option: Step-Up 18PLUS18 Deposits
Type: Locked-in term deposit
Minimum investment: $500
Access: Non-redeemable before maturity.
Fees: None.
Additional information: Offers different interest rates in two periods. First 18 months lower; second 18 months higher.

Option: Tax-Free High Interest Savings Account
Type: Savings account
Minimum investment: None
Access: Any time.
Fees: None, except a $50 fee if the account is transferred to another institution.
Additional information: To withdraw you need go to the bank to sign and allow 24 to 48 hours for processing.

MERIDIAN CREDIT UNION
Area of operation: Ontario
Website: www.meridiancu.ca
Contact phone number: 1-866-592-2226
Options available: Three

Options Offered
Option: Tax-Free Savings Account
Type: Savings account
Minimum investment: $50
Access: Any time. Redeemable and non-redeemable options for term deposits.
Fees: None.

Option: Escalator Term Deposits
Type: Term deposit
Minimum investment: $500
Access: Each anniversary date and 30 days thereafter without penalty. At all other times, this product is non-redeemable.
Additional information: Terms of up to five years with an increase in interest rate each year. Lower rates paid on redeemable term deposits.

Option: Market Secure GICs
Type: Market-link guaranteed investment certificates
Minimum investment: $500
Access: At maturity.
Additional information: Five-year term. The rate of return is based on the performance of the S&P/TSX 60 for a five-year term. Principal is guaranteed. Non-redeemable before maturity.

NORTH SHORE CREDIT UNION
Area of operation: British Columbia
Website: www.nscu.com
Contact phone number: 1-888-713-6728
Options available: Seven

Options Offered
Option: TFSA High Interest Savings Account
Type: Savings account
Minimum investment: None.
Access: One free debit per month as a withdrawal, transfer, or electronic bill payment.
Fees: Average fee of $5 for electronic and in-bank withdrawals.
Additional information: Higher fees for electronic payments.

Option: GuaranteePlus Term Deposit
Type: Market-linked term deposit
Minimum investment: $500
Access: Non-redeemable before maturity.
Fees: None.
Additional information: Principal guaranteed. Performance linked to eight Canadian financial securities. Terms of three and a half or five years.

Option: FlexTerm Deposit
Type: Term deposit
Minimum investment: $100
Access: Redeemable any time.
Fees: None.
Additional information: At maturity you have the option to renew, invest in a different term deposit, or withdraw the funds.

Option: Escalator Term Deposit
Type: Term deposit
Minimum investment: $100
Access: Redeemable on each anniversary date.
Fees: None.
Additional information: Laddered rate over three-year term.

Option: Standard Term Deposit
Type: Locked-in term deposit
Minimum investment: Depends on type selected.
Access: Locked in until maturity.
Fees: None.
Additional information: Inquire about available options.

Option: Long-Term Non-Redeemable Term Deposit
Type: Locked-in term deposit
Minimum investment: $1000
Access: Non-redeemable until maturity.
Fees: None.
Additional information: Laddered rate. Terms of one to five years. At maturity, you have the option to renew, invest in a different term deposit, or withdraw the funds.

Option: Long-Term Redeemable Term Deposit
Type: Redeemable term deposits
Minimum investment: $500
Access: Redeemable.
Fees: None.
Additional information: Laddered rate. Terms of one to five years. At maturity you have the option to renew, invest in a different term deposit, or withdraw the funds.

SERVUS CREDIT UNION
Area of operation: Alberta
Website: www.servuscu.ca
Contact phone number: 1-877-496-2151
Options available: Five

Options Offered
Option: Tax-Free Growth Account
Type: Savings account
Minimum investment: None.
Access: Access any time with no penalty once a year.
Fees: None.
Additional information: $5 for each transaction after first withdrawal.

Option: Long-Term Non-Redeemable GIC
Type: Locked-in guaranteed investment certificate
Minimum investment: $500
Access: Can be redeemed once a year. Locked-in until term is completed.
Fees: None, except for early redemptions fee.
Additional information: Interest paid or compounded annually on anniversary. Terms of one to five years. Interest paid increases each year.

Option: Three-Year Escalator GIC
Type: Locked-in guaranteed investment certificate
Minimum investment: $1000
Access: Can be redeemed once a year.
Fees: None.

Additional information: Three-year term with a guaranteed, escalating rate. Interest paid or compounded annually on anniversary.

Option: Five-Year Escalator GIC
Type: Locked-in guaranteed investment certificate
Minimum investment: $1000
Access: Can be redeemed once a year.
Fees: None.
Additional information: Terms available of five years. Interest rate is paid or accumulated annually on anniversary date. Each year, interest rate increases annually.

Option: Redeemable Rate Builder GICs
Type: Cashable guaranteed investment certificate
Minimum investment: $500
Access: Penalty-free redemption every July.
Fees: None.
Additional information: One-year term. Interest paid or compounded annually.

VANCITY
Area of operation: British Columbia
Website: www.vancity.com
Contact phone number: 1-877-560-0100
Options available: Three

Options Offered
Option: Jumpstart High Interest Savings Account.
Type: Savings account
Minimum investment: None.

Access: Any time.
Fees: None.
Additional information: Investment is connected to Future Foundations program.

Option: Term Deposits (non-redeemable)
Type: Locked-in term deposit
Minimum investment: $500
Access: Non-redeemable until end of the term.
Fees: None.
Additional information: Terms of one to five years. Interest is compounded annually. The rate is fixed for the period of the term.

Option: Term Deposits (Redeemable)
Type: Cashable term deposit
Minimum investment: $500
Access: Cashable at any time, in part or in full, after 30 days without penalty.
Fees: None.
Additional information: Term length is 12 months.

YOUR NEIGHBOURHOOD CREDIT UNION
Area of operation: Ontario
Website: www.yncu.com
Contact phone number: Call local branches listed on website.
Options available: Four

Options Offered
Option: TFSA Savings Account
Type: Savings account
Minimum investment: None.

Access: Any time.
Fees: None.

Option: TFSA High Interest Savings Account with variable rate
Type: Savings account
Minimum investment: None.
Access: Any time.
Fees: None.
Additional information: Tiered account. Higher interest paid on larger balances.

Option: Term Deposits
Type: Cashable guaranteed investment certificate
Minimum investment: $1000 to $2500
Access: After 30 days without penalty.
Fee: None.
Additional information: One-year term at a fixed rate of interest, with a minimum deposit of $1000. Terms from 30 to 364 days, with a minimum deposit of $2500 and fixed rate of interest.

Option: Index-Linked Term Deposits
Type: Market-linked term deposits
Minimum investment: $1000
Access: Non-redeemable until maturity.
Fees: None.
Additional information: Terms available of one to five years. Available only at specific time periods of the year.

Insurance Companies

MANULIFE FINANCIAL
Area of operation: National
Website: www.manulife.ca
Contact phone number: 1-888-626-8543
Options available: Four

Options Offered
Option: Manulife Segregated Fund Contracts
Type: Segregated funds
Minimum investment: $500
Access: Any time at market value.
Fees: Deferred sales charges (DSC).
Additional information: Maturity date December 31 in year annuitant turns 100. Option of paying $100 a month.

Option: Manulife Mutual Funds
Type: Mutual funds
Minimum investment: $500
Access: Any time, minus fees at market value.
Fee: Deferred sales charge (DSC).
Additional information: Option of paying $100 a month for 25 months, providing the contract minimum is met. Also option of paying $100 a month for Simplicity Portfolios.

Option: Manulife Investment GIC
Type: Locked-in guaranteed investment certificate
Minimum investment: $1000 ($5000 contract)
Access: Annuitant's 100th birthday.

Fee: If any money is withdrawn before the maturation of the account, fees will be applied.

Additional information: Offers the option of 30-day "better of" for reinvestments, providing contract of $5000 has been filled. Alternatively, option of paying $100 a month for 25 months for mutual funds. Also offers the option of $100 a month for Simplicity Portfolios.

Option: Tax-Free Advantage Account GIC
Type: Locked-in guaranteed investment certificate
Minimum investment: $2500
Access: The money can be redeemed prior to the maturity of the account but may be subject to market value adjustment and expense recovery fees.
Fees: None except for transfer fee, and expense recovery fee if redeemed early.
Additional information: Manulife Investments Guaranteed Interest Contract (GIC) Basic Non-Cashable Account is not eligible.

15

Your TFSA Questions

At first glance, the concept of Tax-Free Savings Accounts appears to be dead simple. You put money in and then later you take it out, just like with a bank savings account. What could be easier?

But things are not always as they seem, and TFSAs are a lot more complicated than that. I was surprised by the hundreds of questions that flooded my email inbox in the months following the launch of the TFSA program on January 1, 2009. Perhaps it was because people were still trying to come to grips with the new plans, but I suspect it goes beyond that. RRSPs have been around for more than half a century, but I still receive many questions about them each year. The reality is that all government programs come with a lot of regulatory baggage that people have to deal with. Moreover, bureaucrats and politicians have a habit of frequently tinkering with the rules, creating more confusion in the process.

So, if you have questions about Tax-Free Savings Accounts, you can take comfort in the knowledge that you are not alone. Thousands of other Canadians are in the same boat.

This chapter contains some of the questions I have received, divided into subject categories. If you're still puzzled by something, scan through the list of topics and see if you can find the answer to your own question. If not, send it to me at Gordon.Pape@ BuildingWealth.ca and type "TFSA book question" in the subject line. I can't provide personal answers, but replies to selected questions will be posted on www.BuildingWealth.ca and www.TFSAbook.com.

Basic Rules

HOW MANY TFSAs?

Q   I would like to know if I can have more than one TFSA as long as the total contribution to all of them does not exceed $5000 per year?

A   You can open as many TFSAs as you want, just as you can with RRSPs. However, be sure you really need more than one because each account means more paperwork and makes keeping track of the investments more complicated. Also, ask about fees before opening a plan. Some financial institutions have no TFSA administration fees for certain types of plans. A no-fee plan will add to your return.

DELAYING TFSAs

Q   I have two sons in university. I have their upcoming tuition covered with RESPs and in-trust accounts. At this time, they pay no tax because of their tuition deductions, so any money they receive interest on is tax-free. Is it okay to wait and allow them to add to their TFSAs once they are employed (I hope); i.e., can they deposit the $5000 per year "retroactively" when they have the money themselves in future years or do they lose the ability to deposit the $5000 if they do not do it in the year it is eligible?

A   TFSAs have the same carry-forward privileges as RRSPs. It is not a "use it or lose it" situation; if contribution room is not used in a given year, it is added to the next year's limit. So your sons can wait until they have their own cash to open accounts. However, they will lose out on the years of tax-free compounding until then.

TFSAs AS COLLATERAL
Q Can I use my TFSA as collateral?

A Yes. This is one of the major differences between Tax-Free Savings Accounts and RRSPs. The assets within a TFSA may be pledged as collateral against a loan. However, by doing so, you may find that you will be prohibited from making withdrawals as long as the loan is outstanding.

TFSA CARRY-FORWARDS
Q My mom went to a seminar and was told that the contribution room only begins to accumulate after you open a TFSA. That is, if you don't open an account until 2011, you will only be allowed to deposit $5000 because you didn't earn the $10,000 in contribution room in 2009 and 2010. I am wondering whether she is correct (although I will be opening a TFSA in the near future, just to be on the safe side).

A The information she received is incorrect. You don't have to open an account to accumulate contribution room. As long as you are age 18 or older, your TFSA contribution room will be credited to you. If you don't use it, the $5000 will be added to the next year's contribution limit.

If you file an income tax return, the Canada Revenue Agency will keep track of your available contribution room and include the information on each Notice of Assessment you receive, starting in 2010, in the same way as they advise people about available RRSP room. You will also be able to check your contribution room by using the My Account feature on the CRA website.

WHEN DO CARRY-FORWARDS START?

Q   I am not sure if the carry-forward of unused contribution room starts when you open your first account or did it start with the introduction of the Tax-Free Savings Account program itself? For example, if I open my first TFSA account in 2015, will I have a $25,000 contribution limit at that time?

A   Canadians begin accumulating TFSA contribution room at age 18, with 2009 being year one of the program. You don't have to open an account or even file a tax return. Assuming you are age 18 or older now and don't open a TFSA until 2015, as you suggest, at that point you will have accumulated six years of carry-forward room (2009–2014), worth $30,000 using the current annual maximum. Add another $5000 for 2015 and you'll be able to contribute $35,000 that year. In fact, the amount will probably be somewhat higher since the contribution limit is indexed to inflation, although it moves only in $500 increments.

SPOUSAL TFSAs

Q   Can I set up a spousal TFSA? Do I need to? Since the income-attribution rules don't apply, why wouldn't the spouse with money simply give funds to the other to set up a plan in his or her own name?

A   There is no such thing as a spousal TFSA, unlike the situation with RRSPs. Neither are there joint plans. Each person's TFSA is his or her own. So you are correct—one spouse can simply give money to the other to open his or her own plan.

It has been suggested that this creates a way to shift significant assets from one spouse to another over time. For example, a husband might give his wife $5000 to open a plan this year. In December, she withdraws the $5000, which is then added to next year's contribution limit, making it $10,000. He then gives her $10,000 to contribute and the process is repeated annually. On the surface, this would enable her to build a large non-registered investment account as well as a TFSA.

However, the government anticipated this loophole by adding a line that says the attribution rules "will not apply to income earned in a TFSA that is derived from such contributions."[1] Note the phrase "in a TFSA," which suggests that if the money is withdrawn by the spouse and then reinvested, the attribution rules will kick in. We may see a court challenge on this one.

TFSA ELIGIBILITY

Q Thank you for writing the book *Tax-Free Savings Accounts*, which I have read from cover to cover! There is a question I have with regard to eligibility. Our son is a full-time medical student, age 23, a Canadian citizen and a Canadian resident, has a Social Insurance Number, and has filed income-tax returns since he was 18 years old. We wish to open TFSAs for our entire family of four but were recently told by our financial adviser that our son is not eligible, as he is "not a permanent resident" of Canada as he is currently studying in the United States. Please advise! Is he ineligible just because he is temporarily studying in the United States?

A Residency status can be somewhat tricky. However, if your son files Canadian tax returns, does not own property in the United States, and returns to Canada during summer breaks, there is a strong case to be made that he is in fact a Canadian resident. A fact sheet on TFSAs from the Canada Revenue Agency states as follows:

Even if you do not live in Canada, you may have residential ties which deem you to be a resident of Canada. These ties include where your home and personal property are, and where your spouse or common-law partner or dependants reside. Other ties that may be relevant include social ties, a driver's licence, bank accounts or credit cards, and provincial or territorial hospitalization insurance.

The CRA says that additional information can be found in Interpretation Bulletin IT-221R, *Determination of an Individual's Residence Status.*[2]

TFSA PROFITS
Q Suppose I invest $5000 in a Tax-Free Savings Account through a bank using their online brokerage service and I make $2000 in three months on stocks. Can I reinvest the $7000 or can I just reinvest the original $5000?

A As long as you do not withdraw the money from the TFSA, you can reinvest all profits earned within the plan at any time. There are no restrictions.

TREATMENT OF WITHDRAWALS
Q I wanted to use my TFSA to cover monthly bills, followed by topping up when the pension cheque arrives. The man at the bank said that the first time I topped up, the CRA would consider that I had overcontributed and assess a penalty. Presumably, by his reckoning, if a person did this each month, one could wind up with a very sizeable overcontribution at year-end.

Is this guy right? It sounds pretty implausible in these days when the net deposit amount for a given year can be easily calculated and transmitted to CRA should it exceed $5000.

A   Yes, he is correct. Any withdrawals cannot be recontributed to the plan until the following year.

ADVANCE CONTRIBUTIONS

Q   I have already contributed $5000 for this year, and invested in stocks. However, I would like to make another $5000 contribution at this time for the next year. Can I contribute in advance?

A   No. If you contribute any more money to your plan between now and January 1 of next year it will be considered an overcontribution. Any profits made on income earned from overcontributions will be taxed at a rate of 100 percent as a result of changes to the Income Tax Act announced in October 2009.

OVERCONTRIBUTION PENALTIES

Q   The Canada Revenue Agency charges a 1-percent penalty per month or 12 percent a year on overcontributions to the account. But if your yield is higher than 12 percent, I wonder whether the difference is still tax-free? For example: contribution invested to yielding 20 percent per year less 12 percent overcontribution penalty equals 8 percent tax-free yield?

A   That was the case until late October 2009. At that point, Finance Minister Jim Flaherty announced amendments to the Income Tax Act that will impose a 100-percent tax on any profits earned as a result of overcontributions. So forget the whole idea!

MOVING TFSA ASSETS

Q I have a TFSA account with TD Bank and my investment account with TD Waterhouse. Can I move TFSA funds to my general investment account or do these funds have to remain segregated? If the latter, does this mean I need another TFSA account with TD Waterhouse or does the TFSA account with TD Bank need to be transferred?

My example is for TD, but I imagine the question applies to all the big banks with separate investment arms.

A The only way you could move TFSA money into your general investment account is to withdraw it, which I assume is not what you want to do, as you would lose the tax-sheltering.

You could open a new TFSA with TD Waterhouse and transfer some or all of the assets from the bank into it, as there is no limit on the number of plans you can have. However, ask if a transfer fee will apply.

Death and TFSAs

SUCCESSOR ACCOUNT HOLDERS

Q I had an incredibly confusing time designating my husband and I as "successor account holders" for each other's newly opened Tax-Free Savings Accounts. Our broker refuses to allow the "successor" designation to be placed on our accounts. We would greatly appreciate a reply from you clarifying exactly what it is that we can do.

A Succession laws are provincial responsibilities, so although the federal rules clearly allow for a "successor account holder," the provinces each had to pass legislation to actually make it work. Some moved more quickly than others—Ontario, for example, did not implement the needed changes until mid-2009.

All the provinces and territories except Quebec are now onside, but action is required in the case of accounts that were opened before the enabling provincial legislation was passed. In such cases, go back to the plan administrator and complete the necessary documentation.

JOINT TFSAs

Q My wife and I share everything jointly: our real estate, our investments, our bank accounts. Is it possible to open a joint TFSA account? And if not, in the event of the demise of either of us, would the beneficiary (the other spouse) be liable for taxation on the accrued amount?

A Joint TFSAs are not permitted (nor are joint RRSPs for that matter). Each account must be in an individual name. If one spouse dies, the other will acquire the assets tax-free. The most effective way to do this is for each spouse to name the other as "successor account holder."

HUSBAND DIED, BANK CONFUSED

Q My husband passed away on May 17, 2009. He has a TFSA with our bank. The chequing and savings accounts are now in my name. It seems that my bank does not know what to do with his $5000. Any ideas?

A My condolences on your loss. It sounds like he did not designate you as a successor holder or beneficiary before he died. Perhaps this was because your province of residence had not approved enabling legislation.

The assets in the plan should pass to you tax-free nonetheless, but they might have to be processed as part of his estate, depending on the laws in your province. You should speak to a lawyer who specializes in this field.

TFSA BENEFICIARIES

Q How does survivorship affect the TFSA, if you include children and spouse as beneficiaries in the TFSA account or through a will? Are there any probate fees to be paid?

A Succession laws are governed by the provinces, so the situation will depend on where you live. However, in all provinces except Quebec, you can now designate a spouse/partner as a successor account holder, which you should do. This ensures the assets in a TFSA will pass to the spouse/partner without having to wait for the estate to be settled and with no probate fees. Do not designate your spouse and children as joint beneficiaries, as that could create some legal problems.

General Strategies

SWITCHING TFSAs

Q I would now like to switch from a high-interest savings account to having some U.S. dividend–paying stocks in the account. Is it as simple as closing the existing account and setting up a self-directed TFSA or are there special rules/penalties surrounding this sort of change?

A You need to be careful if you have already made your maximum TFSA contribution for this year. If you withdraw the money from the account, you will not be able to recontribute it until January 1 of next year. At that time, the withdrawal will be added to next year's contribution allowance.

However, you can transfer the money directly into a new plan at the same financial institution, if it offers a brokerage service, or another one without running into this problem. There may be a fee for closing the existing account.

But are you sure you really want to do this? Gena Katz, executive director, Tax Practice, at the accounting firm of

Ernst & Young, says that the United States does not recognize TFSAs as registered plans when it comes to withholding tax on dividends. That means that 15 percent of all U.S. stock dividends paid into a TFSA will be withheld at source. (RRSPs and RRIFs are exempted from this withholding under the Canada–U.S. Tax Treaty.)

Maybe you should think this through again.

BALANCING ACT

Q   I work on contract. Currently, my income stream is fine until the contract expires in September. I can always try to get contract work again, although it is not guaranteed. I wonder about my priorities in managing my finances. Should I build my cash reserve, make an RRSP contribution, or make a lump-sum payment against my mortgage? I have cash for four months of living expenses right now.

A   Given the uncertainty of your situation, I suggest adding to your cash reserve. You may want to consider opening a Tax-Free Savings Account and keeping your emergency money there so as to eliminate taxes on the interest. Just make sure you don't lock in to a GIC in case you need to withdraw money.

If your employment situation becomes more stable, you can then withdraw some of that TFSA cash and make an RRSP contribution. Use the refund it will produce to make a mortgage payment. Yes, it's a balancing act, but it works.

NEEDS TFSA MONEY FOR DAUGHTER

Q   My husband and I opened two individual TFSAs, depositing $5000 each. Since then we have found out that our daughter has been accepted in a post-graduate program. We did promise to her a while back that we would help her out with tuition. Now the question is, Can we withdraw some of the funds at the beginning of each semester and apply the proceeds against her tuition and reinvest the same amount prior to the year-end? For instance, this year we would withdraw money from the TFSAs in September and by December we will redeposit the same amount in the same TFSAs, repeating this procedure semester after semester.

A Sorry, your plan won't work. You are allowed to replace the money you withdraw from a TFSA but not until the next calendar year. If you redeposit the cash in December, it will be considered an overcontribution and you'll be faced with a tax of 100 percent on any profits earned from that extra money.

USE TFSA TO PAY MORTGAGE?

Q I am wondering if it would be strategic to invest $5000 in a TFSA now, withdraw the total funds in December, and put the proceeds against my mortgage. Next January, I would invest $10,000 in my TFSA and in December withdraw the total amount to pay against my mortgage, repeating this strategy year after year.

A This approach makes sense only if the rate of return you achieve within the Tax-Free Savings Account is higher than the interest rate on your mortgage. For example, if your mortgage rate is 4.5 percent but you can earn only 3 percent within your TFSA, you would be better off applying the $5000 against the mortgage principal immediately rather than waiting.

Finding the Money

TFSA SAVINGS

Q We are very intrigued by Tax-Free Savings Accounts—savings with no strings attached. But to contribute $5000 each per year (so a total of $10,000) would require a contribution of approximately $833/month. I'm not sure how we would find the financial resources to do that. How would you recommend going about this?

A Most Canadians receive an income tax refund each year. If you are among them, use that money to start a TFSA for each of you. That will reduce the additional monthly contribution you need, perhaps significantly.

Investment Options

RETURNS ON TFSAs

Q We've done some research but couldn't find any institution offering a competitive rate of return on a TFSA. Most are offering a maximum of 3 percent, so how would we get close to a 6-percent average rate of return?

A You're operating under the assumption that the money in a TFSA must be invested in some type of deposit account. That is not the case. TFSAs are like RRSPs in that there are several different types of plans. If you want to aim for a higher rate of return, choose a plan that allows you to invest in mutual funds or a self-directed plan that enables you to buy almost any type of security. You may not have to invest in the stock market to earn a 6-percent return—there were some good-quality corporate bonds that were paying yields in that range at the time of writing.

LOOKING FOR CERTAINTY

Q If we aim for a 6-percent return, can we be certain that the 6-percent interest rate would stick for the course of 20 to 25 years?

A You can't be certain of a 6-percent return, certainly not in the form of interest payments. These days, you're lucky to earn

4 percent on a five-year GIC. But you can expect to average at least 6 percent over the long haul by investing in a good-quality balanced fund or buying some high-grade corporate bonds.

TFSAs AND GICs

Q   On page 42 of *Tax-Free Savings Accounts* you state, "Avoid GICs or any other security that locks you in for long time." I had a GIC that became redeemable. I saw my investment adviser at the bank and asked that this GIC be transferred into a TFSA. She advised me not to do this but rather to reinvest into the same GIC so that I would not have to pay the interest. Somewhere in your book you advise to transfer your GICs, pay the interest, and deposit to a TFSA. I would appreciate your comments as to which is the best solution.

A   The advice about not putting a GIC into a Tax-Free Savings Account related to using a TFSA as an emergency source of cash, a "rainy day fund" if you like. Holding a GIC in such a situation means you cannot get at the money if it is needed, so the whole emergency fund idea is defeated.

It is perfectly all right to invest in a GIC inside a TFSA as long as you understand that the money is locked in until maturity. So for conservative, long-term investors, a GIC is an option to consider.

Regarding your GIC that recently matured, I do not see what the problem is. The interest you earned is taxable—that's clear. You can now take the cash from the redeemed GIC, deposit it into your TFSA (to your contribution limit), and invest in a new GIC inside the plan if that is your wish. The interest earned on the new GIC will be tax-sheltered within the TFSA.

SAVING FOR RETIREMENT

Q Do you have any specific advice/guidelines on what type of vehicles/recommended fund groups to hold in my Tax-Free Savings Account? I am a 42-year-old, married, self-employed mother of two. I plan to use all funds in my TFSA as part of my retirement plan. Thank you for any guidance.

A My first comment is that you should probably make the maximum contribution to your RRSP before using a TFSA for retirement savings. You'll get a tax deduction for the RRSP, which a TFSA will not give you.

If you have done that, I suggest taking a conservative approach with your TFSA investments since this money is, in effect, part of your personal pension plan. Since the annual contribution limit is only $5000, it can be expensive and inefficient to try to create a diversified portfolio immediately. Therefore, I suggest you start with a low-risk balanced fund. After a couple of years, when the assets in the TFSA have grown, you can blend in a range of other securities if you wish.

MAWER FUND

Q What is your opinion of the Mawer Canadian Balanced Retirement Savings Fund as an initial $5000 TFSA holding for a conservative growth investor? The component equity funds are all highly regarded, the component bond fund appears to be middle of the pack, and the MER is low.

A This is a fund of funds, meaning that it invests primarily in six other Mawer funds with the Mawer Canadian Bond Fund as the largest single holding. The Calgary-based Mawer organization is a boutique house that I have recommended for several years. The firm received the 2009 Lipper Award as the best equity fund company in Canada.

This particular fund is slotted into the Global Neutral Balanced category where it has been an above-average performer for all time frames from one to 20 years. I think it would be a fine TFSA choice for a low-risk investor.

WHERE TO INVEST?

Q   I have money in a U.S. index fund. The amount I have exceeds $5000. I was thinking of putting $5000 in a Tax-Free Savings Account. My question: If I do open this type of account, do I have to contribute each month or could I make a one-time deposit of $5000 and just let it grow through interest? If I do this, what is the interest per month? One other question: Will I earn more by moving my money from a U.S. index fund to a TFSA or should I leave my money in the U.S. index fund? I am not really sure which is the better investment.

A   There is clearly still a lot of confusion about what TFSAs really are. That's not surprising—the same thing happens with RRSPs and they have been around for more than 50 years.

To be clear, TFSAs, RRSPs, and so on are *not* investments. They are simply tax-sheltered "boxes" into which you place investments. When you open a TFSA or an RRSP, it is empty. You then fill it with whatever you want, as long as the investment is allowed by the Canada Revenue Agency.

So this is not a choice between a U.S. index fund and a TFSA. You can move $5000 worth of fund units *into* a TFSA, provided you set up the right kind of plan. In this case, it appears a self-directed TFSA with a broker would be the most appropriate.

You do not have to make monthly contributions. You can deposit $5000 cash or make a "contribution in kind" of $5000 worth of fund units. But a word of caution: If your fund has lost money, don't do a direct transfer, as you will not be able to

202   The Ultimate TFSA Guide

claim a capital loss. Sell $5000 worth and deposit the cash. Then you can claim a loss when you file your next return.

You asked about the interest rate for a TFSA. That depends on what type of interest-bearing investment you choose, if you decide to switch from the U.S. index fund. If you don't want to stay in the fund, check around for options.

TFSA RATES

Q What is a usual interest rate banks offer for a TFSA?

A There is no "usual" rate. It depends on the type of plan and the financial institution you are dealing with. If you have a savings account type of TFSA, the current interest rate will be minimal. It should rise when interest rates generally move higher but that may not be for some time. If you invest in a GIC, the rate will depend on the term and the type of GIC (redeemable or non-redeemable). A market-linked GIC will carry no fixed interest rate. Also, smaller institutions usually offer better rates. Shop around.

Remember, a TFSA does not have to come with any interest rate. It depends on the plan and how you invest. If you choose a mutual fund plan or a self-directed plan, no interest rate will apply.

YOUNG PERSON WANTS TO GET STARTED

Q I am turning 22 soon and would like to start investing for retirement, buying a house, and paying off student loans. I want to invest $2000 to start and would like to withdraw the money in 10 years at the earliest.

I've talked with financial planners/investment specialists at Coast Capital Savings, BMO, TD, Scotiabank, and Royal Bank. However, I have found that they all offer similar mutual funds that charge about the same MERs.

I am an aggressive investor (based on these financial institutions' questionnaires) and would like to maximize capital gains for the long term. Are there any specific mutual funds you recommend to be put in a Tax-Free Savings Account? Since I have only $2000 to invest right now, should I buy one or two mutual funds?

A Congratulations for understanding the importance of starting a savings program early. However, you may want to begin with an RRSP rather than a Tax-Free Savings Account because of the tax deduction the former will generate. Take a close look at the two options before you decide.

In either case, you should keep your costs as low as possible at the outset. Normally, I would recommend a self-directed plan for an aggressive young investor. But the annual fee would be out of line with the amount of money you have available. Therefore, I suggest you begin with a no-fee mutual fund plan from one of the financial institutions you have talked to.

My advice is to start with a high-quality balanced fund and put the $2000 into that. Then, as you add more money to the plan, buy other funds for diversification. Once you have $15,000 invested, switch to a self-directed plan at a brokerage firm that will give you more investment options.

TFSAs FOR OLDER PEOPLE

Q I have just finished reading your book on Tax-Free Savings Accounts (TFSAs). Very informative and easy to understand. My question: You gave examples of how couples can become millionaires. Great, but what does a 70-year-old widow do to achieve similar status? I did start a TFSA this year and have investments in mutual funds, GICs, and so on. How do I position myself to get the best results? Thank you for paying attention to those of us who don't want to leave all our money to the governments!

A I wish I could promise that you, too, could become a million-aire with your TFSA, but unless you plan to live until about 110, I really can't. It takes time, especially given the low annual contribution limit of $5000.

However, you can use your plan to maximize your tax-exempt investment earnings for as long as you live. The best way to achieve that is to hold securities that you expect to generate the most taxable profit inside your TFSA. These would normally be stocks or mutual funds, especially in this low–interest rate environment.

Let's say you have a choice between investing in a GIC that pays 2.5 percent and a stock that you expect to gain 10 percent over the next year. For every $1000 invested in the GIC, you would shelter $25 annually in interest. The stock would generate a capital gain of $100 for every $1000 invested. Half of that ($50) would be taxable outside a TFSA. So you double the tax-sheltering value of the plan by holding the stock in the TFSA. Of course, that involves more risk, but your question was how to get the best results.

DOUBLING YOUR TFSA

Q I opened my $5000 TFSA account with one of the banks in January 2009. The interest paid started out at 4 percent and is now reduced to about 1 percent. I do not know where to invest to get the best rates. Could you please give me a few great options from which to choose? One of your readers wrote the following, which I thought was rather amazing: "After making a $5000 contribution to my TFSA this spring, I have managed to build it to $12,000." Thank you.

A Obviously, our reader did not build $5000 into $12,000 by putting his money into a savings account or a GIC. Although he did not tell us how he managed to more than double his

TFSA assets in a few months, he probably opened a self-directed plan and invested in stocks when the market was down in early 2009. He didn't have to buy penny mining stocks to do it. An investment of $5000 in Bank of Montreal shares on February 24, 2009, would have been worth $11,350 in early August of that year, not including dividends. There are many other examples of blue-chip stocks more than doubling in that period.

Of course, there is more risk in investing in the stock market. People have to decide for themselves whether they are willing to accept that. If you want to stick with low-risk, interest-bearing investments, the best rates are usually offered by smaller financial institutions. But a word of warning: Before you decide to move your TFSA somewhere else for a slightly higher return, ask whether any transfer or account-closing fees will be charged. They would probably exceed any additional interest you would earn for the next year. And don't expect to double your money any time soon by sticking with a savings account or GIC.

RRSPS and TFSAs

RRSP TRANSFERS
Q Can I transfer funds from my RRSP to a TFSA?

A This question came up many times. The answer is no, and if you think about it for a moment the reason is obvious. RRSP contributions generate a tax deduction. The offset is that you pay tax when the money comes out of the plan. TFSA withdrawals are tax-free. So if you were allowed to shift money from an RRSP to a TFSA, you would end up having a deduction going in but paying no tax coming out. The government may have been in a generous mood when it created TFSAs, but not that generous.

TFSA OR RRSP?

Q Would you say that TFSAs are becoming a better way to invest than RRSPs? I have both, at 62, no dependents and no personal debt. Would bank preferreds go into either one?

A It's not a matter of one being "better" than the other. They're both excellent savings vehicles. Which one should get priority depends on your personal situation.

As a general rule, if you expect your income to be lower after retirement than it is now, contribute to an RRSP first. That's because your tax rate now is higher than it will be after you stop work. Your refund will therefore be greater than the amount of tax you'll be assessed when the money is withdrawn from the plan.

If you expect your income to be higher after retirement (perhaps because of a generous pension plan or an anticipated inheritance that will be invested), then use the TFSA first.

You can put bank preferreds into either plan provided it is self-directed. However, you will lose the benefit of the dividend tax credit by doing so.

RRSP WITHDRAWAL STRATEGY

Q I am 62 and retired. My taxable income for 2008 was just over $24,000, around $14,000 below the threshold where I would have gone up to the 22 percent income tax bracket from 15 percent. This is actually a two-part question. I have approximately $400,000 in an RRSP that I don't expect to need until I must convert to a RRIF at age 71. Is there a case to be made for withdrawing $5000 from my RRSP and investing the money in a TFSA or is it better to leave the money in the RRSP until I must withdraw it? My tax accounting is simple enough that I can fairly accurately calculate for tax purposes the monetary difference between the lowest (15 percent) tax bracket and the next higher bracket prior to year-end, if I wanted to withdraw the maximum amount up to the 15 percent threshold.

I have enough capital outside my RRSP that I am able to put the allowable $5000 into a TFSA account for the next eight years, without using my RRSP money.

A Your last sentence tips the balance here. If you did not have the money available outside the RRSP for a TFSA contribution, I would have said your logic makes sense. But you do, so it doesn't. The goal of any investor should be to minimize taxes. This means tax-sheltering as much money as you can for as long as you can. The money in the RRSP is already tax-sheltered. The capital outside the plan is not so you will pay tax at the marginal rate on any investment income it earns. Therefore, your best strategy is to shelter as much of that capital as possible by using it to make a maximum TFSA contribution each year.

You did not mention a spouse, but if you have one you can give her $5000 each year to open her own plan, thereby doubling the tax-sheltered amount.

WHERE TO DRAW MONEY?
Q In the next two to five years, my wife and I will be funding our retirement from CPP/OAS, a small pension, non-sheltered investments, TFSAs, and RRSPs. For tax efficiency, I assume we should draw down from our non-sheltered investments first (to supplement CPP/OAS and pension income). However, once those funds have been exhausted, will it be more tax efficient to draw down from the TFSAs or RRSPs first?

We loaded up our TFSAs with blue-chip, dividend-generating equities that should provide a dividend stream and (hopefully)

long-term capital gains that can continue to grow completely
tax-sheltered in the TFSAs. If these same investments were
made in the RRSP, the dividend income and capital gains would
eventually be taxed on withdrawal as if they were interest
income. But these TFSA benefits will be short-lived if we have
to draw down from the TFSAs first (recognizing that our non-
sheltered investments will run out in a few years).

A   I would leave the money in the TFSAs and draw down the
RRSPs. Here's why.

Let's suppose you have $5000 investments in each plan
earning 7 percent annually. Five years from now, that investment will be worth $7012.76. Now you are faced with a
withdrawal decision. If you take the money from the RRSP,
using a marginal tax rate of 30 percent, you will be assessed
$2103.83 on the withdrawal. That will leave you with a net,
after-tax return of $4908.93. Note that is less than the value of
the original $5000 investment, which means that all the
income you earned over the five years and more went in taxes.
By comparison, a TFSA withdrawal will be worth the full
$7012.76—you keep *all* the investment income.

This example does not take into account the benefit of the
tax refund you received for the RRSP contribution, but that is
in the past. What you are concerned about now is realizing the
highest after-tax return from invested money that is already
tax-sheltered. Leaving the TFSAs intact is the best way to do
that.

Taxes and TFSAs

WANTS TO CLAIM A LOSS
Q   I transferred 600 trust fund units valued at $5000 to my TFSA
from a non-registered account. They increased slightly in value

and I sold them recently at a considerable loss from my original purchase. Can I still use this capital loss against my capital gains in the non-registered account it was transferred from when filling out my tax return?

A It sounds like you have made a classic and costly mistake. Based on your question, it appears that your units were already in a loss position before you moved them to the TFSA. In that case, you lost the right to claim a capital loss when you transferred them.

With TFSAs, as with RRSPs, the rules are that when an asset is transferred into a plan from a non-registered account it is deemed to have been sold for tax purposes. Any capital gain is taxable and must be declared on your next return. But, and here is the kicker, capital losses are not recognized in this situation and cannot be claimed. You should have sold the shares instead of transferring them and deposited the proceeds in the TFSA. That would have crystallized the loss for tax purposes. There is nothing you can do now, unfortunately.

FUTURE TAX RATES

Q I read the section in your book *Tax-Free Savings Accounts* about the scenarios of which choice would be better between contributing toward an RRSP and a TFSA. To recap,

1. If the tax rate after retirement is expected to be the same as it is now, TFSAs and RRSPs will produce the same net after-tax result.
2. If the tax rate after retirement is expected to be less than it is now, it is better to top up an RRSP before opening a TFSA.
3. If the tax rate after retirement is likely to be higher than it is now, saving in a TFSA will produce a better return than making an RRSP contribution.

Now the million-dollar question is, Where do you feel tax rates will be 10 years in the future compared to present?

A   Talk about crystal ball gazing! The obvious answer is, Who knows? Most governments in recent years have recognized that lower tax rates encourage higher employment and greater economic activity. Offsetting that are the large deficits that were incurred in creating the stimulus programs to combat the recession. Many economists believe that without tax increases, those deficits will continue for years to come.

On balance, my guess is that governments will first try to close the deficit gap by raising sales taxes, including the imposition of the harmonized sales tax (HST) in those provinces where it does not already apply. Higher federal income taxes would be a last resort but can't be ruled out. If they are required, lower- and middle-income wage earners would likely face very small increases with upper-income earners bearing the most of the financial burden.

WILL TFSA DIVIDENDS BE TAXED?

Q   I just finished reading your book and I have one question: Assume I invest $5000 by buying a bank stock with a good dividend yield. If the stock value is unchanged at year-end, but I received some dividend payments giving me a total value in my TFSA account at December 31 of, say, $5200, will I be penalized? I know that if the stock value increases we are okay, but do I have to allow for dividend or interest or distribution payments when calculating my maximum?

A   No worries. All profits earned inside a Tax-Free Savings Account are tax-free, regardless of their source—capital gains, dividends, or interest. The only way you risk putting yourself in an overcontribution situation is if you deposit more than your annual contribution limit into the plan.

CLAIMING A CAPITAL LOSS

Q   If I sell a stock in an unregistered account and generate a capital loss, can I still claim this capital loss if I immediately repurchase the same stock within a Tax-Free Savings Account?

A   No. The "superficial loss" rule would apply. This states that if you, an "affiliated person," or a trust you control buys the same stock "during the period starting 30 calendar days before the sale and ending 30 calendar days after the sale," no capital loss can be claimed. TFSAs fall under the "trusts" designation. See the Capital Gains Guide published by the Canada Revenue Agency for more details.[3]

U.S. DIVIDENDS

Q   My income is low enough that I do not usually have to pay income tax, but I still have withholding tax deducted from any U.S. dividends. Would it be a good idea to hold U.S. dividend-paying equities in my TFSA?

A   Under the Canada–U.S. Tax Treaty, U.S. dividends paid in an RRSP or RRIF should not have any tax withheld at source, although I have heard from some readers that this rule is not uniformly applied.

TFSAs are not covered by the Canada–U.S. Tax Treaty, which deals with such issues. Nor are they likely to be in the future, as they are not technically "retirement savings plans." The bottom line is that any tax withheld from U.S. dividends paid to TFSAs will be lost. In this specific instance, TFSAs are not "tax-free."

16

Yes, You *Can* Be a Millionaire!

TFSAs can make you a millionaire! Not in one year, or five, or even 10. But if you're young enough and stay with the plan, it is certainly an attainable goal. When you combine TFSAs with RRSPs, it's almost a sure thing, providing you can save enough and you invest wisely.

Of course, being a millionaire isn't what it used to be. Fifty years ago, a millionaire was someone who could live like royalty. These days, it's anyone who can afford to drive a car! Well, that's overstating the case, but many families who have mortgage-free homes and some savings put aside are probably getting close to millionaire status.

Nonetheless, the idea of being a millionaire remains a financial dream for many people. TFSAs will make that dream easier to achieve, but you will still need discipline and investment acumen to bring it all together.

In my book *6 Steps to $1 Million*, I wrote that there are two tracks to great wealth. One is to create it through hard work and innovation. The other is to save it. The new TFSAs are part of the savings track.

Let's look at four fictional couples and see how each might gain millionaire status with TFSAs and how quickly it could happen.

Sean and Alison: Slow and Steady

We'll begin by considering the situation of Sean and Alison, who live in Halifax. They are both 25 years old and were married last year. Alison inherited the family home after her mother died, so they are living mortgage-free. This enables them to save more than most young people their age.

Both of them had made RRSP contributions before the wedding and invested in mutual funds. They were shocked when they discovered that their retirement plans had lost 40 percent in the stock market meltdown of 2008–2009. After that, they decided "never again." In the future, all their money would be put into safe securities such as GICs. They both understand this will reduce their potential returns, but that is a price they are willing to pay for peace of mind.

Both Sean and Alison opened TFSAs on January 2, 2009, and contributed the $5000 maximum. The money was invested in five-year GICs. They intend to continue doing this for the foreseeable future, increasing their contributions as the limits rise. Over the years, as interest rates rise and fall, they expect an average annual return of 5 percent.

How long do you think it will take them to accumulate a million dollars between them in their TFSAs at this slow but sure savings rate? Would you believe they will have reached that goal by the time they are 56 years old? That's right—assuming that inflation runs at 2 percent a year and contribution limits increase as per the existing law, even a low-risk investment program can make a young couple millionaires well before their normal retirement age. This table shows their progress.

How Sean and Alison's TFSAs Grow

Years	Contribution limit (per person)	Period-end TFSA value
2009–2011	$5000	$33,101
2012–2016	$5500	$106,068
2017–2020	$6000	$183,233
2021–2024	$6500	$281,555
2025–2027	$7000	$372,276
2028–2031	$7500	$520,389
2032–2034	$8000	$655,377
2035–2037	$8500	$814,953
2038–2039	$9000	$937,230
2040	$9500	$1,004,042

Assumptions: Maximum contributions are made at start of year. Inflation rate is 2%. Average annual return is 5%.

Anil and Sujata: Buying Blue Chips

Anil and Sujata live in Regina. He is 43 and she is 42. They have two children, both of whom are now living away from home. They jointly run a successful hardware store. Their mortgage is paid off. However, the cost of raising a family and paying for their house has left them with no retirement savings. Now they want to remedy that.

Because they had no investments, they weren't hurt by the market collapses of 2002 and 2008. But many of their friends were. They don't want the same thing to happen to them, but they also realize that because they have no money put aside for retirement and they have a relatively short time frame, they will have to take more risk if they are going to be able to sell the business and retire when Anil reaches 65.

Together, they decide that, considering the circumstances, the best strategy is to use their TFSAs to invest in a portfolio of blue-chip stocks. They realize that the markets will continue to fluctuate over the years, but they believe that by dollar-cost averaging their investments over a long period of time, they will be able to achieve an average annual compound rate of return of 8 percent, including dividends. Can they achieve their million-dollar objective by 2031? Let's take a look.

How Anil and Sujata's TFSAs Grow

Years	Contribution limit (per person)	Period-end TFSA value
2009–2011	$5000	$35,061
2012–2016	$5500	$121,212
2017–2020	$6000	$223,306
2021–2024	$6500	$367,071
2025–2027	$7000	$511,490
2028–2031	$7500	$768,875
2032–2034	$8000	$1,024,569

Assumptions: Maximum contributions are made at start of year. Inflation rate is 2%. Average annual return is 8%.

The answer is, not quite. Under these assumptions, their combined plans will be worth about $770,000 in 2031. But if they continue on the same course for another three years, when Anil will be 68, they'll achieve the million-dollar plateau.

Of course, if they save money in an RRSP as well, they'll reach a million dollars easily, and much sooner. If they each contribute $10,000 a year to an RRSP (assuming they have enough earned income to do so), their plans will be worth almost $990,000 after 20 years, again assuming 8 percent annual growth. Add that to the TFSAs and they are well beyond the million-dollar mark. And here's the kicker: If their marginal tax rate is 35 percent, their RRSP contributions will generate tax refunds of $3500 each (or $7000 for the two of them), which will cover a large portion of the TFSA contributions. This is a good way to make both plans work in tandem.

David and Rebecca: Rolling the Dice

David is a stockbroker and Rebecca is a chartered accountant. They are both very savvy about money and investing, and they are determined to get as rich as possible as quickly as they can. They understand the risk involved, but because they don't plan to have children, they are prepared to live with that. David is 32 and Rebecca is 30. They live in Montreal.

David knows all the tricks of the brokerage trade. He knows how to use options, how to leverage investments through exchange-traded funds, and how to play market cycles. He understands the investment rules governing TFSAs and is convinced he can operate within them to generate an average annual return of 15 percent on their money. A target this high is extremely aggressive and requires active management of the account and a lot of intestinal fortitude. David believes he can do it, and Rebecca supports him.

They decide they are going to push their TFSAs to the limit in their investment choices. He reviews the portfolios at least once a day, buying and selling regularly. He buys energy stocks when oil is cheap and sells when crude spikes higher. He trades in and out of gold shares. He buys exchange-traded funds that pay off double when the indexes they track move in the right direction.

Most of the time, it works. Like all investors, David suffers some setbacks along the way, but they are more than offset by years in which he is able to double the money in the plans. Over time, he achieves his 15 percent average annual goal. So let's see how much money David and Rebecca end up with.

How David and Rebecca's TFSAs Grow

Years	Contribution limit (per person)	Period-end TFSA value
2009–2011	$5000	$39,934
2012–2016	$5500	$165,612
2017–2020	$6000	$358,565
2021–2024	$6500	$701,784
2025–2027	$7000	$1,123,233
2028–2031	$7500	$2,050,677
2032–2034	$8000	$3,182,717
2035–2037	$8500	$4,908,402
2038–2039	$9000	$6,535,867

Assumptions: Maximum contributions are made at start of year. Inflation rate is 2%. Average annual return is 15%.

By the time David turns 50, their combined TFSAs have passed the million-dollar level, but he's just getting started. Compounding works like a snowball rolling downhill, rapidly increasing your savings in size as it goes. It takes only an additional four years or so to add another million to the pot. By the time he is 60 and Rebecca is 59, their TFSAs have accumulated almost $5 million, all tax-free. They'll be able to retire very comfortably on that money, although David will probably want to keep on going. He's the type you'll see in the library of a cruise ship, following the markets via satellite internet as he and Rebecca tour the world.

Jenny and Paul: Small Savings Add Up

Of course, many families will not be able to put aside enough money to make a maximum TFSA contribution. The budget is stretched thin just keeping up with household expenses; there's hardly anything left over at the end of the month.

Jenny and Paul are in that position. The 22-year-old Winnipeg couple are living common law for now, although they intend to marry within two years. They both work at modest-paying jobs, she as a library assistant and he as a trainee bus driver. They have no children but intend to start a family someday.

They like the idea of opening TFSAs, but they realize that they won't be able to contribute much, at least at the start. So they make a deal. They'll begin by putting $1000 a year each into their plans. Every five years, they'll add another $500 to the amount. They will invest the money in balanced mutual funds, which they hope will return an average of 7 percent annually. Here's what happens as the years pass.

How Jenny and Paul's TFSAs Grow

Years	Annual contribution (per person)	Period-end TFSA value
2009–2013	$1000	$12,307
2014–2018	$1500	$35,720
2019–2023	$2000	$74,713
2024–2028	$2500	$135,555
2029–2033	$3000	$227,043
2034–2038	$3500	$361,513
2039–2043	$4000	$566,267
2044–2048	$4500	$835,572
2049–2053	$5000	$1,233,466

Assumptions: Contributions are made at start of year. Inflation rate is 2%. Average annual return is 7%.

This one is an eye-opener! Even starting with very modest contributions and investing in moderate-risk balanced funds, Jenny and Paul are able to build their combined TFSAs to a value of more than a million dollars by the time they are 65 (the actual amount in the plans at the end of the year in which they celebrate their 65th birthdays will be $1,142,772).

So even young people who don't have a lot of money can use these plans to create significant personal wealth if they are willing to make the commitment.

If you want to check out how TFSAs can work most effectively for your family, Scotiabank has created a useful online calculator that demonstrates how quickly your tax-free savings will grow. You can plug in any assumptions you wish, including initial lump-sum contributions, monthly contributions, various rates of return, and time horizons. It's available at www.scotiabank.com/tfsatool.

A Tax-Free Future?

Tax-Free Savings Accounts were really created out of political expediency. As we saw in Chapter 1, Finance Minister Jim Flaherty had painted himself into a corner when it came to presenting his 2008 budget. Having given away everything that was left in the store in his Economic Statement the previous October, he badly needed something to showcase in February after the anticipated election failed to materialize. TFSAs fit the bill and the immediate cost to the Treasury was minimal.

As it turned out, no one gave the Conservatives much credit for TFSAs in the election campaign that took place in the fall of 2008; in fact, they were barely mentioned. But now they're here, and at some time in the future another finance minister may look back and ask, "Why?"

As the years pass, the amount of money invested in TFSAs will reach hundreds of billions of dollars. Some economists are already predicting that the time will come when many older Canadians will pay no taxes at all while at the same time drawing heavily on government programs such as OAS and medicare.

Whether this will be sustainable is something that future governments will have to decide. It is not inconceivable that at some point, we may see a freeze on TFSA contributions or a tax on the withdrawal of investment earnings, albeit at a reduced rate.

But all of that is problematic, and if any changes are made to the system, it won't happen for many years. For now, Canadians have an extremely valuable new savings program with which to build their personal fortunes. Make the most of it!

Action Summary

1. Make your TFSA contributions at the start of each year to maximize tax-sheltered growth.
2. Decide on an investment strategy that suits your temperament and financial knowledge. Even a low-risk approach will enable a couple to accumulate a million dollars in their plans if they have enough time.
3. You don't have to be well-off to build wealth in a TFSA. Even if your income is modest, open an account and keep adding to it. Remember, the original reason why the C.D. Howe Institute promoted these plans was that they are an effective savings option for lower-income people. The younger you are when you start, the more effectively they'll work for you over time.

Notes

1: The Beginning: Budget 2008

1. The Honourable James M. Flaherty, P.C., M.P., minister of finance, *The Budget Speech 2008*, Department of Finance Canada, February 26, 2008. Available at www.budget.gc.ca/2008/speech-discours/speech-discours-eng.asp.

2. Ibid.

3. Julie Smyth, "Budget Report Card," *National Post*, February 26, 2008. Available at http://network.nationalpost.com/np/blogs/posted/archive/2008/02/26/budget-report-card.aspx.

4. Benjamin Tal, "The New Tax-Free Savings Account: How Popular Will It Be?" *Consumer Watch Canada*, CIBC World Markets, September 11, 2008. Available at http://research.cibcwm.com/economic_public/download/cwcda-080911.pdf.

5. Steven Chase, "Small Change for Tighter Times," *The Globe and Mail*, February 27, 2008. Available at www.theglobeandmail.com/servlet/story/RTGAM.20080227.wbudget27/BNStory/budget2008/home.

6. Rob Carrick, "A Place to Park Cash but Not the Break They Promised," *The Globe and Mail*, February 27, 2008. Available at http://v1.theglobeandmail.com/servlet/story/RTGAM.20080227.wbudgetcarrick_new0227/BNStory/budget2008.

2: Some History

1. Department of Finance, *The Budget Plan 2004*, Annex 9. Available at www.fin.gc.ca/budget04/pdf/bp2004e.pdf.

2. "What Constrains Flaherty's Budget," *The Globe and Mail*, February 18, 2008. Available at www.theglobeandmail.com/servlet/story/RTGAM.20080218.wxebudget18/BNStory/specialComment.

3. William B.P. Robson and Finn Poschmann, *Steering Through Turbulence: The Shadow Federal Budget for 2008*, C.D. Howe Institute, February 2008. Available at www.cdhowe.org/pdf/backgrounder_111.pdf.

4. Conservative Party of Canada, Platform 2004, *Demanding Better.* Available at www.theglobeandmail.com/bnfiles/politics/2004/Conplat form2004.pdf.

5. Conservative Party of Canada, Platform 2006, *Stand Up for Canada.* Available at www.scribd.com/doc/334166/Conservative-Party-of-Canada-Federal-Election-Platform-2006.

6. Benjamin Tal, "The New Tax-Free Savings Account: How Popular Will It Be?" *Consumer Watch Canada,* CIBC World Markets, September 11, 2008. Available at http://research.cibcwm.com/economic_public/download/cwcda-080911.pdf.

7. HM Revenue and Customs, *ISA Rules Are Changing.* Available at www.hmrc.gov.uk/ISA/rule-change-april08.htm.

8. HM Revenue and Customs, *ISA Bulletin Number 14–25 June 2009.* Available at www.hmrc.gov.uk/isa/bulletin14.htm.

9. Richard Shillington, *New Poverty Traps: Means Testing and Modest-Income Seniors,* C.D. Howe Institute, April 2003. Available at www.cdhowe.org/pdf/backgrounder_65.pdf.

10. Finn Poschmann and William B.P. Robson, *Saving's Grace: A Framework to Promote Financial Independence for Low-Income Canadians,* C.D. Howe Institute, November 2004. Available at www.cdhowe.org/pdf/backgrounder_86.pdf.

11. John Stapleton and Richard Shillington, *No Strings Attached: How the Tax-Free Savings Account Can Help Lower-Income Canadians Get Ahead,* C.D. Howe Institute, September 2008. Available at www.cdhowe.org/pdf/ebrief_64.pdf.

3: The Basic Rules

1. Survey, Polls & Research, "Scotiabank Study Confirms Canadians Seek More Information on the Tax Free Savings Account," November 6, 2008. Available at www.duedee.com/news/367797/Scotiabank-study-confirms-Canadians-Seek-More-Information-on-the-Tax-Free-Savings-Account/print.

2. Richard Shillington, *New Poverty Traps: Means Testing and Modest-Income Seniors,* C.D. Howe Institute, April 2003. Available at www.cdhowe.org/pdf/backgrounder_65.pdf.

5: Rainy Day TFSAs

1. Statistics Canada, *The Daily,* September, 15, 2008. Available at www.statcan.ca/Daily/English/080915/d080915a.htm.

6: TFSAs or RRSPs: Which to Choose?

1. Department of Finance Canada, *The Budget Plan 2008*, Annex 4. Available at www.budget.gc.ca/2008/plan/ann4a-eng.asp.

2. James Daw, "Teachers Take Pension Cutback," *Toronto Star*, October 1, 2008. Available at www.thestar.com/Business/article/509241.

3. Richard Shillington, *New Poverty Traps: Means Testing and Modest-Income Seniors*, C.D. Howe Institute, April 2003. Available at www.cdhowe.org/pdf/backgrounder_65.pdf.

7: Tax Relief for Seniors

1. Canada Revenue Agency, *2009 Interim Statistics (2007 Tax Year)*, Table 4. Available at www.cra-arc.gc.ca/gncy/stts/gb07/pst/ntrm/table4-eng.html.

2. Julie St-Arnaud, Marie P. Beaudet, and Patricia Tully, *Life Expectancy*, Health Reports, Vol. 17, No. 1, Statistics Canada, November 2005. Available at www.statcan.ca/english/studies/82-003/archive/2005/17-1-e.pdf.

8: Education Savings

1. A.J.C. King and W.K. Warren, *Transition to College: Perspectives of Secondary School Students,* Social Program Evaluation Group, Faculty of Education, Queen's University, 2006. Available at www.collegesontario.org/research/school-college-transition/CO_TRANSITION_COLLEGE_FULL.pdf.

9: Save Taxes by Splitting Income

1. Ernst & Young, 2009 Personal Tax Calculator. Available at www.ey.com/CA/en/Services/Tax/Tax-Calculators-2009-Personal-Tax.

2. Department of Finance Canada, *The Budget Plan 2008,* Annex 4. Available at www.budget.gc.ca/2008/plan/ann4a-eng.asp.

3. Department of Finance Canada, Tax-Free Savings Account Calculator. Available at www.budget.gc.ca/2008/mm/calc_e.html.

10: Passing On

1. Ernst & Young, 2009 Personal Tax Calculator, Available at www.ey.com/CA/en/Services/Tax/Tax-Calculators-2009-Personal-Tax.

11: Tax-Saving Strategies

1. To illustrate, suppose you buy a mutual fund at $10 a unit and receive an ROC distribution of $0.40. Your ACB will be $9.60 ($10 − $0.40 = $9.60).

2. Rates as per 2009 tax year. In the 2008 budget, the federal government announced it will reduce the amount of the gross-up and the tax-credit percentage in three stages from 2010 to 2012 to reflect reductions in the corporate tax rate.

3. Mackenzie Financial Corporation, Tax and Estate Planning Team, Tax-Free Savings Accounts (TFSAs), 2008. Available at www.mackenziefinancial.com/eprise/main/MF/DocLib/Public/TF5906.pdf.

15: Your TFSA Questions

1. Department of Finance Canada, *The Budget Plan 2008,* Annex 4, *Attribution Rules.* Available at www.budget.gc.ca/2008/plan/ann4a-eng.asp.

2. Canada Revenue Agency, *Interpretation Bulletin IT-221R, Determination of an Individual's Residence Status.* Available at www.cra-arc.gc.ca/E/pub/tp/it221r3-consolid/it221r3-consolid-e.pdf.

3. Canada Revenue Agency, *Capital Gains Guide 2008.* Available at www.cra-arc.gc.ca/E/pub/tg/t4037/t4037-08e.pdf.

Acknowledgments

This book and its predecessor, *Tax-Free Savings Accounts*, could not have been written without the help and co-operation of many people. The whole concept of TFSAs is still very new, and even now all the nuances of these plans are not apparent. I have asked several experts in the field of tax and personal finance to assist me in sorting out the intricacies of these plans and all have been very generous in sharing their knowledge.

I would especially like to acknowledge the contributions made by the following:

Sandy Cardy, vice-president of Tax and Estate Planning Service for Mackenzie Financial;

Jason Enouy, senior manager, Process & Regulatory Solutions, Scotiabank Wealth Management;

Jamie Golombek, managing director, Tax and Estate Planning, CIBC Private Wealth Management;

Gena Katz, executive director, Tax Practice, Ernst & Young; and

William B.P. Robson, president and CEO of the C.D. Howe Institute.

I would also like to thank the staff of the federal Department of Finance and the Canada Revenue Agency, who handled all my many queries and followed up with the answers in time to meet my tight deadlines. The people in our public service don't get enough recognition for efforts such as this, so I'm taking this opportunity to say a heartfelt "thank you."

Special thanks to my chief researcher (and daughter), Kim Pape-Green, who tackled the difficult job of pulling together detailed information about the TFSA programs offered by financial institutions across Canada, and to my granddaughter, Kendra Pape-Green, who assisted in compiling and editing the material. Kim also prepared the endnotes and the index, operating (as we all were) under intense time pressure to meet the publishing deadlines.

Of course, this book would not have been possible without the support and encouragement of my long-time editor, Andrea Magyar, and her team at Penguin Group Canada. Special thanks also to production editor Sandra Tooze and my copy editor, Heather Sangster.

All these people worked together as a team to make this book possible. No writer can function without them. Thank you.

For More Investment Information

Sleep-Easy Investing

Gordon Pape's bestselling book *Sleep-Easy Investing: Your Stress-Free Guide to Financial Success* is available in a paperback edition from Penguin Group Canada.

Sleep-Easy Investing is a must-read in these turbulent times. In it, Gordon Pape offers a totally new approach to investing, one that will take the anxiety out of your financial decisions while still enabling you to earn good returns. He describes the philosophy outlined in the book as a "health trumps wealth" approach to sensible money management.

The book is filled with personal anecdotes, real-life emails from investors in trouble, and down-to-earth, practical advice on how to succeed without stress. "This book looks at investing from a human perspective rather than as an exercise in numbers," says Gordon Pape. "Over the years I have come to realize that financial experts sometimes forget that human psychology is the most important factor when it comes to investing success and personal wealth. I think this book will completely change the way many people feel about investing—for the better!"

Sleep-Easy Investing is available at bookstores across Canada.

Newsletters

Gordon Pape is the editor and publisher of several investment newsletters. They include,

The Income Investor. This twice-monthly newsletter focuses on income-generating securities with the goal of providing readers with above-average returns consistent with reasonable risk. At a time when interest rates are low and income trusts are being phased out of existence, the guidance provided by this newsletter is vital to anyone seeking steady cash flow from their investments.

Internet Wealth Builder. This weekly email newsletter covers all aspects of investing and money management, including stocks, bonds, mutual funds, income trusts, taxes, and general economic comment. The seasoned team of contributing editors includes some of Canada's best investment minds. The newsletter takes a conservative approach to money management and was among the first to warn of the drop in the Toronto Stock Exchange in a lead article published in mid-June 2008, just a few days after the TSX hit an all-time high.

Mutual Funds Update. Now in its 16th year of publication, this monthly newsletter continues to represent the gold standard in sound, sensible mutual funds advice. One of its most popular features is the Ideal Portfolios, which provide models for investors of all types, from ultra-conservative to growth-oriented.

For information on these newsletters, visit www.Building Wealth.ca or call toll-free 1-888-287-8229.

Websites

More financial information from Gordon Pape can be found at the following websites.

www.BuildingWealth.ca offers free investment articles, a Q&A feature, valuable free budget and net worth spreadsheets, book excerpts, and more.

www.TFSAbook.com contains more information about Tax-Free Savings Accounts and how to use them most effectively.

Index